hum♥r
for a
w♥man's heart 2

Stories, Quips,
and Quotes
to Lift
the Heart

HOWARD
®PUBLISHING CO.

Compiled by Shari McDonald
Illustrated by Dennis Hill

Our purpose at Howard Publishing is to:

• *Increase faith* in the hearts of growing Christians
• *Inspire holiness* in the lives of believers
• *Instill hope* in the hearts of struggling people everywhere

Because He's coming again!

Humor for a Woman's Heart 2: ISBN: 0-7394-3998-7

Compiled by Shari MacDonald
Cover art by Dennis Hill
Illustrated by Dennis Hill
Interior design by Stephanie Denney

Contents

chapter 4: making humor your hobby

chapter 5: queen of domesticity

chapter 6: looking fine, feeling foolish

chapter 7: clutter bugs unite!

chapter 8: laughter for the chronologically challenged

chapter 9: technology: friend or foe?

chapter 10: a pound of laughter

chapter 11: mama mia—more humor for moms

chapter 12: adolescent amusement

chapter 13: funny honeys

chapter 14: man-oh-man:
laughing with the guys we love

chapter 15: what do women and cheese
have in common? we both age well

chapter 16: just when you thought it was safe to stop laughing

chapter 17: kids: God's way of making sure we laugh—especially at ourselves

contributors—221

source notes—225

laugh and the whole
world laughs with you...
or is it at you?

Bless Our Thighs

When my son, Tony, was asked to say the prayer for the offering one night at church, he was a little nervous. It was obvious when he asked everyone to bow their heads, then proceeded to pray, "Lord, bless us as we bring you our thighs."

—MARTHA BOLTON,
LIVING IT DOWN BY LAUGHING IT UP

When a Chicken Goes to Church

Gracie Malone

Traditionally, the first day of the week is a day of rest. Not so for a chicken who wants to look her Sunday best when she goes to church; sometimes just "putting on my face" is too much for this old hen to handle.

On a recent Sunday morning, I awoke with a headache and was barely into my second cup of coffee when the clock warned: Time to get dressed. I donned my best denim outfit, cleansed my face with cold cream, dabbed skin freshener into my pores, and began the painstaking process of applying makeup.

I applied moisturizer, concealer, foundation, pink blush, two shades of taupe eye shadow, and a thin line of dark brown eyeliner. Then I loaded the mascara brush with dark brown mascara, applied one coat to the topside of my lashes, and started on the underside, when, for reasons unknown, I blinked. Poked that tiny brush-looking thing straight into my eye. In an effort to

keep tears from spilling over onto my freshly made face, I tried bugging my eyes and glaring at the ceiling—to no avail.

Salty tears ran down my cheeks, washing brown goop into all the wrinkles around my eyes, filling the bags underneath. When my vision cleared to the point where I could fully assess the damage, I saw I'd also managed to paint a large, brown "Z" on my eyelid.

Quickly, I dipped a Q-tip into eye-makeup remover and gingerly tried to lift the brown stuff without disturbing the makeup layers underneath. It didn't work. I ended up with a bright spot of white where taupe should have been. Streaks of gray marred my perfect pink blush. There was no recourse but to start all over again.

I cleansed my face with cold cream, dabbed on some skin freshener, applied moisturizer, concealer, foundation, pink blush, two shades of taupe eye shadow, and a thin line of brown eyeliner. Loading my mascara brush with dark brown mascara, I once again—oh so carefully—applied one coat of mascara to both sides of my lashes. Then I slicked on some lipstick, washed down two Tylenol with a cold sip of coffee, and gathered my purse, keys, Bible, and notebook. Finally, I headed out the door.

Since I was running so late, I practically flew my little car to town, careened into the parking lot, and ran lickety-split toward the worship center. Once I hit the foyer, I paused to gather my dignity, straightened my dress, and pasted on my best Sunday-go-to-meetin' smile. Just as the organ prelude ended, I walked circumspectly into the auditorium and found a seat next to my good friends, Mike and Linda. Whew! Was I ever ready for a few quiet moments of spiritual worship.

Halfway through the call to worship, I spotted a dear hen friend, Carolanne, standing in the back. She was loaded down with her purse, a box of Sunday school literature, and a Bible big enough to choke a mule. I motioned for her to join us.

The first hymn began, and since Carolanne wanted to avoid drawing attention to herself, she decided to squeeze into the space at the end of the pew next to Mike. But how could Mike have known what Carolanne was planning to do? He assumed she would want to sit next to the girls—Linda and me. So instead of scooting to his right to make room for her, Mike stood in gentlemanly fashion and stepped out into the aisle.

I could see that Mike and Carolanne were on a collision course and tried in vain to get Mike's attention. The two collided in a most inappropriate manner. Carolanne let out a big whoop and whirled around. Mike grabbed her arm to steady himself, and for a few moments, it looked like they were dancing in the Baptist church and, of all things, to the tune of "What a Friend We Have in Jesus."

They were dancing in the Baptist church—and to the tune of "What a Friend We Have in Jesus."

"Oh, 'scuse me," Mike muttered as he sat down and started to make room for Carolanne where he now thought she wanted to sit—near the end of the pew. But, by this time Carolanne had changed her mind. I don't know what possessed her to enter the pew facing the three of us. While still clutching the armload of books, she stepped across Mike's knees at the precise moment he started to scoot over. I don't think I've ever seen a woman in such an awkward position, especially in

church. There was no way she could have prevented what happened next.

Carolanne dropped that box of Sunday school literature right on Mike's lap. He let out a low groan that caused all eight members of the Mayo family seated in front of us to turn and gaze. Carolanne tried to retrieve her box, but Mike grabbed it and plopped it beside him while muttering, "Just sit down, over there, please." Then he shook his head and added, "I'm glad I've already had my family."

As Carolanne settled between Linda and me, she kept repeating, "I'm so sorry. I should have sat on the end of the pew." By this time everybody around us had lost their composure. As we stifled our giggles, the pew shook so hard I thought the bolts anchoring it to the floor would pop loose. As I dabbed my eyes with a tissue, I noticed my mascara was coming off again.

We finally gained control and joined with boisterous enthusiasm on the next hymn. After the last stanza, I peeped over Carolanne's shoulder and asked Linda, "Is Mike OK?" She whispered, "I think he finally caught his breath"—a simple comment that sent us into another round of hysteria.

For the rest of the service, Mike sat straight as a rail with his hands clasped in his lap. But there was a silly grin on his face, and every once in a while, he'd whisper another funny observation that would have the entire pew shaking with laughter again.

At the end of the service, I could not recall one thing I'd heard from the sermon and yet, strangely, I felt so good inside. Throughout the day and into the next week the flush of joy remained in my heart. On Monday I ran into Carolanne in the grocery store and we laughed one more time. On Friday Linda told me Carolanne had sent Mike a get well card.

Sometimes I wonder, *What's church all about if it's not about enjoying friends, sharing real moments of genuine laughter, fellowship, singing praises, and caring about each other?* Those are gifts from God that make this chick kneel on both drumsticks and worship.

I have to admit, going to church is worth all the trouble of "putting on my face"—even if I do end up crying (or laughing) it all off again!

The One enthroned in heaven laughs.—Psalm 2:4

Hens and Neighbors, Gather 'Round

Fran Caffey Sandin

"Mom," my daughter had told me, "you might really enjoy using a round brush when you blow dry your hair. They're great for adding body and bounce." Since my medium-length hair is an odd combination of thick and fine, I was open to suggestions.

The next time I went grocery shopping, guess what? I was thrilled when I found a cute, small, round brush, for the discounted price of 99 cents. Since I love a good bargain and could envision my hairstyle undergoing a glamorous transformation, I grabbed the beauty tool from the marked-down basket and hurried home to give it a whirl.

As soon as I walked into my kitchen, I plopped down the bag of groceries, turned on the radio and began humming. While putting cans away in the pantry, I ran across my new purchase and thought, *I wonder how this brush works?* Right where I stood by the kitchen counter, I reached up, grabbed a bunch of hair

from the top of my head, and tucked the strands into the bristles of the tiny brush. Then I began winding. And winding. And winding—while musing, *Hmm, this is just like rolling spaghetti on a fork.* I was amazed at how many turns I could make.

But I was even more surprised when I discovered the brush that had so beautifully wound up my hair, now refused to let go. I flew into the bathroom, hoping a mirror would help me see a way to release my locks from the evil contraption. I pulled and tugged in all directions. My efforts only succeeded in tightening the tangles. My chicken heart skipped a beat as I imagined being stuck with this bonehead attachment forever—like Pebbles from the Flintstones!

Then I remembered my hen friend, Gracie, who lived only a few blocks down the street. Quickly, I dialed her number. When she answered I stammered, "Gracie, are you my friend?—my *really good* friend?"

"Sure," she said reassuringly, "what's wrong?"

"Well, is it okay if I come over—like, right now?"

"Yes, but what's the matter?"

"You'll know when you see me." When I hung up the phone, I felt a combination of urgency and relief. I ran out the door, jumped into the car, and raced toward Gracie's house like some hair-brained woman.

Considering my delicate condition, I was hoping no one would see me. But while rounding the corner, my hopes were dashed. There stood a rather dignified-looking lady in her designer jogging suit. As I drove by, there was little I could do but smile and wave at her. From my rearview mirror I watched her head slowly swivel in my direction, a look of shock rising on her face. I tried to reassure myself, *Maybe she'll think I'm starting a new trend—"brush-roll-n-go."*

The minute I pulled up to Gracie's sidewalk, she flung open her front door and immediately began laughing. Stepping out to meet me she asked, "What have you done to yourself?"

I didn't know whether to laugh or cry so I scooted inside, closed the door and blurted, "Help! Gracie, this is serious. What am I going to do? I cannot get this brush out of my hair! I have pulled and jerked in every direction, but the brush keeps on taking wrong turns. Can you work on it? Please? I know you can do it. I have confidence in you, Gracie. Please."

"Well, let me get the scissors," Gracie quipped with a twinkle in her eye.

"Oh no! That's what Jim would do."

After a pause of playful hesitation, Gracie said, "You poor, pitiful chick. Have a seat at my kitchen table."

Gratefully, I scooted my chair into place as I fondly thought, *Gracie and I have shared many cups of tea and talked each other through so many ups and downs around this table.* Now here I was in the middle of yet another situation I simply could not handle without my friend and neighbor.

With the tender-loving care of a mother hen, Gracie began the arduous task of unwinding the mess of matted hair, strand by strand. After 15 or 20 minutes of concentrated effort, punctuated by outbursts of laughter, Gracie triumphantly declared, "TA DA!"

Then she sang out, "Here's your lovely hairstyling accessory," as she showed me the brush. It looked like a hamster that had been caught in a whirlwind.

I grabbed the beastly brush and asked Gracie, "Where's the nearest trash can?"

Thankfully, only one part of my hair stayed with the bargain brush. I touched the top of my head and found some remnant.

Breathing a sigh of gratefulness, I gave Gracie a big hug and promised I would "be there" if she ever needed me to do anything. Ever. At all.

Later as I reflected on my emergency I thought how thankful I was to have Gracie as my neighbor. What would I have done without her? Then I began thinking about how important it is for us to reach out, especially to those who live around us.

Before the days of air-conditioning, folks spent time on their front porches, often chatting with their neighbors. Most activities revolved just around the church and the school instead of the myriad of "extracurriculars" which now bombard us. Hens had quilting bees; roosters helped each other build fences and barns. Now, in our mobile society and insulated houses, we have to make an extra effort to get to know our neighbors.

Sometimes I am so busy with my own "to-do" list, I fail to be a good neighbor. But when I do take the time, it helps me capture warm feelings of community. I begin to have compassion for the struggles of others. There are so many ways to show concern. Sometimes all it takes is a telephone call, stretching a recipe to have an extra plate of warm, homemade goodies, or even just sharing a good book.

Here I was in the middle of yet another situation I simply could not handle without my friend and neighbor.

My brush with "the brush" taught me just how important it is to develop relationships before a crisis occurs (not to mention buying a large round brush). No matter how independent we think we are, there'll be times when we desperately need someone who cares (and is even willing to "de-brush" our hair).

Love your neighbor as yourself.—Matthew 19:19

Loony 'Tudes

Patsy Clairmont

Dictionary's definition: Strange and unusual.
Patsy's definition: My kooky comrades.

I'm convinced that the Lord, who created us in His own image, laughs. And I'm certain He meant for us to laugh until we cry as an emotional safety valve. He knew life would pile up inside us, and a sense of humor would help us shovel our way out of our serious circumstances. At times, laughter must be as sweet an offering to Him as tears and even prayers.

My mom and her sisters didn't believe in foolishness, but they sure believed in a good time. They worked hard and laughed hard. I always looked forward to being with them, even as a child. The smell of down-home cooking and the sound of good-hearted laughter were an unforgettable combination.

I have been blessed to have not only a heritage and a husband of humor, but also a passel of loony 'tude friends. They've helped

me survive when life knocked the humor out of me or when I took myself too seriously. Laughter puts life back in its temporal position, lest we think our earthly stint is all there is to this journey. Also, shared laughter leads to an emotional connection with others.

I remember attending a large conference where I noticed a couple of my long-lost friends seated in a row near the front. I decided to join them, which meant I would have to climb over several of them to reach the empty seat. That didn't seem to be a problem—and probably wouldn't have been had I not gained weight.

Forgetting I would need more clearance than in my slim past, I began to slide my body across their laps in an attempt to reach the vacant chair. Well, I made it past Marita, but when I crossed over Becky's lap, the space narrowed, and I didn't. I ended up stuck. Or more accurately, my backside was stuck. And I do mean stuck! Becky had papers, program, and purse in her lap, and somehow I became entangled and Becky became ensnared. The straps of our purses were looped around each other and the chair, tying us securely. We couldn't pull apart the straps or us. I couldn't move sideways or up, and she couldn't move over or back. The more I pulled and tugged, the tighter we became cinched together.

I was now perched on Becky's aerobically thin lap. Both of us were restricted in movement, and to add to our dilemma, we became tickled. The enormous room was fairly dark. That was good. But we were surrounded by thousands of people, and we didn't want to distract them or cause a ruckus. But honestly, we couldn't help ourselves. Becky was laughing so hard she was gasping for air. (That or my added tonnage had knocked the breath

right out of her.) I, confused about how I had become permanently affixed to my friend, began to titter. My tittering turned
to jostling as my repressed giggles transformed my cellulite body
into a human vibrator. I shook so vigorously that I dislodged
Becky's papers that had been between us, and they fluttered to
the floor. That minute space gave us a little leeway, and with a
mighty jerk, I rolled into the empty seat next to my mushed
buddy.

We looked at each other, our outfits now askew from our tug-
of-war, and we lost it. Tears cascaded down our faces while the
arteries in our necks grew alarmingly swollen. Marita looked at
us, baffled. She wondered what could possibly have been that
funny about our scuffle.

It was one of those times when you not only had to be
there, but you also had to be actively involved to understand
our reaction. It was unexplainable, but gratefully it was
expressible through laughter. Becky and I did gain a wisp of
composure but found it necessary to avoid eye contact until
after we left the arena, lest we set each other off. Because Becky
and I shared deeply an emotion, it added a fun memory to our
friendship, enhancing it.

Recently our friends David and Nancy joined Les and me for
a northern Michigan, cottage-on-the-lake adventure. They flew
in from California for a time of relaxation and fellowship. What
we hadn't anticipated was that when the summer residents had
moved out of the cottage we were to stay in, Mickey, Minnie,
and several namesakes had moved in.

Signs of their intrusion were, *eek,* everywhere. The invading
troops had shredded sugar packets, powdered-cream packets, and
tea bags for nesting material. They had set up housekeeping in

the pots and pans, and one resident was building a condo in a stove burner. She must have decided on a Southwest decor, because she had dragged in a five-inch feather to enhance her surroundings. And of course a profusion of mouse confetti (if you know what I mean) was sprinkled throughout the premises to announce their ownership of the establishment. It was their little way of claiming squatters' rights, and it was obvious they had been doing that very thing.

Well, it's like this, folks: I don't do mice. No how, no way. I was on my way out the door, headed for higher ground, when the others convinced me we could win against these little varmints. Les and David started the cleanup campaign, while Nancy diverted my attention with the beauty of our surroundings. Then we went to town and bought traps. Lots of traps. Scads of traps. And we placed them all around the house.

That evening we were playing Jenga, a nerve-racking game of building a tower one log at a time, when a trap went off. I almost ate my log. The guys yelled, "All right!" Then they gave each other a high-five victory slap, acting as if they just struck oil. Nancy and I cried, "Oh, no! Yuck!" Then the big-game hunters went to examine their prize. We heard one say to the other, "Oh, cool. Look at how squished he is. Hey, girls, wanna see?"

What is it about guys and guts, anyway? And why do they love to gross out girls? Talk about loony 'tudes!

The trap snapping continued throughout our four-night stay. The guys were thrilled at the sound of each snared tenant, and we girls were nauseated. In the mornings, Les would say to David, "We'd better check our trap lines." You would have thought they were snaring a bear. Afterward, David and Les were sorry they hadn't taken a picture with all their prey dangling between them on a clothesline. They really are a couple of Mouseketeers.

Despite my passionate dislike for those little fur balls with feet (the mice, not the guys), we had great fun. In fact, I'm almost certain that without the little creature-feature, we wouldn't have had such a hilarious adventure. Although...

David, Nancy, Les, and I took a trip out east two years ago, staying at bed and breakfasts, seeing the breathtaking autumn scenery, and eating ourselves silly. The farther east we traveled, the more signs we noticed alerting us to moose traffic. Other than Bullwinkle, I'd never seen a moose up close and personal. We were all vigilant in hopes of being the first to spot a moose. Then one day David suddenly let out a yelp. "A moose! A moose!" he repeated in his excitement. His flailing arms pointed back to a road we had passed.

Les, who's always up for an adventure, did a dramatic U-turn and headed pell-mell for the sighting. He careened the van head-long into the road, and there, facing us, was the biggest, fattest barrel you'd ever want to see. Did we ever laugh! Oh, my, all our sides were splitting. Well, David wasn't laughing quite as hard as the rest of us. So for the remainder of the trip, we took turns yelping at barrel sightings just to make David feel better.

Now that I think about it, it wasn't the mice or the moose that added to our vacations. Instead, it was our loony 'tude friends who make fun a part of their everyday lives.

Have you ever noticed how some people seem to have a greater capacity for fun and laughter than others? Do you think it's in the genes? Or do you think they purpose to find the good, the positive, and the humorous? Hmm, it might be worth a try.

the mother of all laughs
—humor for moms

I Had a Lot to Learn

As a young mother, I asked the Lord to teach me of Himself and of myself through my children. He gave me eight children. Apparently, I had a lot to learn.

—HELEN WIDGER MIDDLEBROOKE,
LESSONS FOR A SUPER MOM

You Know You're Really a Parent When...

Susan Friday Lamb

When does that magic moment come when you realize you're a bona fide parent? You'll know it for sure when:

12. You eat dinner on dinosaur-decorated placemats.
11. You catch yourself singing the "Barney" theme song—in public.
10. You stop the tears by taping broken crayons back together.
9. You long for nothing more than a good night's sleep.
8. You buy jelly according to the characters on the jar.
7. You know the best way to scrape dried Cheerios off the floor.
6. You find out you never have to buy another Christmas ornament.
5. You share the storage closet with a miniature broom and vacuum cleaner.
4. You take phone messages in crayon.

3. You always buy the big pack of batteries—but you can never find one when you need one.

2. You find action figures in your washing machine.

1. You find yourself cutting your spouse's meat into bite-sized pieces.

Paging Dr. Mom

Charlene Ann Baumbich

Last day of school. This mother's delight—and torment. Delight that the nightly homework hassle is behind us for a few months, and parts of our harried schedule can take a nap. Torment because my last day of personal freedom until fall is drawing to a close.

There's a decision to be made here: should I be busily cleaning on this last of child-free days for a while? Nah. I should be sitting in the back yard amongst the flowers, sipping tea, reading or just staring into space. And that's precisely what I do.

I ponder the fact that Bret is experiencing his final day as an eighth grader. Major transitions lie ahead, for him and for me. For Bret, manhood looms around the corner. But first he must pass through another transition fire: going from being the eight-grade hot shot to once again ranking lowest on the totem pole in a different school. As for George and me, we must help keep his

self-esteem intact during this stormy period as well as allow him some room to be an adolescent—a difficult stage for everyone involved.

It also occurs to me I can no longer simply say what grades my boys are in when queried; I must refer to them as "a third grader and a freshman in high school."

Freshman! What year is this? I prop my tea glass in the grass next to my lawn chair and head for the bathroom mirror. After a couple minutes of jowl and crows' feet inspection, I decide things aren't too bad yet. Besides, why waste these precious moments worrying anyway? I resume my laid-back post.

While I am watching cloud formations, Bret is manning home plate during a softball game at school. Steve Wasnick is pitching. There is a play at the plate. Wasnick whips the ball to Bret who immediately drops it because pain shoots through his thumb the second the ball smacks into it.

The runner is safe. Bret is sent to the nurse. She deems it possibly broken. School is almost out for the day, however, so she ices it for a while, advises him to be careful of his throbbing digit and ride the bus home as usual. Of course he is to tell his mother that she, the nurse, believes his thumb should be x-rayed. Upon his arrival home, he does so, abruptly ending my freedom.

Before I deal with the thumb, however, I quickly thank God for the wisdom he granted me to know when it was time to stockpile a refreshing little rest instead of scurrying around spit-shining. I just love it when daydreaming wins! Especially when it beats out ring-around-the-collar calisthenics. "Thank you, God," I say, "for this profound discovery!" Now, back to the hand in my face.

I carefully inspect his thumb, the way I have inspected dozens

of other injured limbs of both my children over the years. It looks slightly swollen, but then so do his eyes. So does a sprain. So does a mosquito bite or a good wallop.

He sighs as he reads my mind, the mind he has eventually heard spoken every other time this scenario has played.

"How badly does it hurt?" I always ask them. "It's probably not broken. We'll just go sit in the clinic for hours while they shuffle us from urgent care to x-ray and back again," I whine. "Then the doctor will finally tell us nothing is wrong and we will receive a very large bill and by tomorrow you will forget it even hurt." Not once has anything actually been broken.

But we always go anyway because I don't know what a broken anything really looks like, and my conscience starts riding me, and I love my children and I don't want them to heal with crooked limbs.

"It's probably not broken. The doctor will tell us nothing is wrong and we will receive a very large bill."

For the record, it has also been proven that I do not consistently know the difference between postnasal drip and bronchitis. How many times, I wonder, has Brian snorted and snotted around, running a slight temperature on and off, keeping us (mostly me) up at night, only for us (always me) to become convinced he will surely die without some of that pink medicine. And so I sit next to my phone in the early hours with bleary eyes haunting the clock, waiting for the appointment lines to open.

Off we finally go. Sometimes we get pink medicine or a shot. During these times I commend my intuitive self. Except, of course, for the time I sent him to school after a check-up and a

throat culture because he had no temperature and seemed perfectly fine but for a scratchy throat. And don't you know the lab called and said it was strep!

But other times we are informed of a mere cold, postnasal drip, or less. And we pay our bill. And I file the episode in my memory bank for the next bout. Just like I file the "nothing-is-broken" messages we've always received. Try chicken soup and Popsicles first, I tell myself. Wait a couple days and see what transpires, I coax.

But now, this last-of-eighth-grade day, Bret stands before me, thumb presented like a royal jewel to a queen. I express my sympathy and look appropriately sad. He still thinks it's broken. I soften my usual lecture. He sighs again and endures, but doesn't become dissuaded. I wear down and take him to the clinic.

I can't say I was happy, but somehow I was momentarily justified as a mother.

After the predicted waits between shufflings, we finally watch the doctor ceremoniously mount two very large black-and-white bits of evidence on a lighted screen. He carefully studies them, moving his head between the two. Next, he pulls a ball-point pen out of his pocket.

"Right here," he says, using the pen for a pointer, "is a slight fracture. We'll get a splint on that and it should heal just fine."

Bret jumps up in the air and screams, "Did you hear that, Mom? It's broken! It's really broken!" He grins from ear to ear as he dances around me celebrating, right there in the doctor's office. A doctor, who, I might add, seems a bit puzzled at the reaction.

I can't say I was happy, but somehow I was momentarily justified as a mother. A mother who made the right move this particular day.

And there was another happy person: Steve Wasnick. The next day Bret ran into him at a carnival. When Bret confirmed the implications of the metal and green-foam splint he was wearing like a medal of honor, the two of them did a high five. Wasnick was overjoyed that he could throw a ball fast enough to break someone's thumb!

Even Brian was happy. Although he got no immediate pleasure out of the ordeal, he knew that from this day forward he would have something to remind Mom about the next time she started her "I'm-sure-it's-nothing" lecture.

A Jiggling Box of Joy
LeAnn Weiss

When Barbara returned from shopping, she knew immediately by the laughter and commotion in the kitchen that her sons were up to something. But walking into the kitchen, she couldn't believe her eyes. Her four boys, ages sixteen to eight, were sitting at the table using spoons to fling the raspberry Jell-O with banana chunks, which she had made earlier that day, at her formerly spotless white brick kitchen wall. It was obvious that her oldest son, Tim, who was supposed to maintain order while she was gone, was the ringleader.

The shrieks of exhilaration and accompanying sound effects from the flying red missiles hitting the wall came to an abrupt halt when the boys realized their mother's presence. The silence was deafening as they awaited their sentence. Each of them mentally prepared their last wills and testaments as their mom stood

shaking her head in disbelief. They knew that this caper was going to test even her sense of humor.

As Barbara stared first at the wall and then at the boys, they just knew she was debating whether to scream, faint, spank, ground them for life, or kill them. They were caught red-handed.

But realizing that the kids were going to have to clean up the mess anyway, Barbara finally responded, "Where's my spoon?"

Shocked but relieved that his mother was joining their escapade, Tim handed her the biggest cooking ladle he could find. After watching their mom send several ladles full of Jell-O and bananas beaming at the wall, the boys breathed a collective sigh of relief. Then for the next fifteen minutes, the five of them slung red globs of Jell-O together, laughing hysterically all the while. By the time they ran out of ammunition, the entire wall was a sticky red mess.

> Each of them mentally prepared their last wills and testaments as their mom stood shaking her head in disbelief.

Of course, Barbara supervised as her boys spent the next two hours scrubbing down the wall and kitchen floor. More than thirty years later, Barbara still chuckles that God gave her the foresight to transform the raspberry caper into a memory the Johnsons will never forget. They still laugh each time they see Jell-O commercials, having experienced the true fun found inside that small box.

3

laugh your way to a better figure

All Things Beautiful

Our preacher told us "All things are beautiful in God's eyes," which was enough to get me to go off my diet.

—GENE PERRET,
ON THE 8TH DAY...GOD LAUGHED

Who Me? Sweat?!?

Lynn Bowen Walker

What woman doesn't harbor secret guilt, knowing she should be pumping those steel buns if she wants to stay healthy and embody peak physical form? But who among us actually looks forward to squeezing into those outstretched exercise pants and heading down to the local gym to sign up for eight weeks of leg cramps and breath deprivation?

Here are a (Baker's) Dozen Questions To Ask Yourself Before Signing Up for That Aerobics Class. If you end up with mostly yeses, prepare to glow.

1. Can I face my children, after droning on about peer pressure, with my $40 exercise outfit that ensures I am clad just like all the other ladies?

2. Can I ignore the inner chastising of my 13-year-old son who says my at-home dancing "embarrasses him in his own kitchen," as

I strut in a room full of strangers flapping my arms like a chicken and lifting my leg in a decidedly dog-like maneuver?

3. Can I commit to a one-hour class when just wriggling into my exercise bra leaves me winded?

4. Is my faith big enough to encompass Spandex?

5. After complaining about hauling stray shoes and laundry up and down the flight of stairs at home, can I in good conscience actually pay someone to order me on and off a step 367 times?

6. Can I bark in rhythm? ("Who let the dogs out? Woof. Woof. Woof. Woof.")

7. Can I maintain my dignity when I discover I am prancing east while the rest of my class parades west?

Can I commit to a one-hour class when just wriggling into my exercise bra leaves me winded?

8. Can I convince anyone that it really takes a minute and a half to retie my shoe in the middle of the Latin Salsa routine?

9. Can I exhibit love, joy, peace, and patience while refraining from tattling on the woman in front of me who's cheating at thigh squats?

10. Can I resist the temptation to compare butt sizes with the 20-year-old next to me who's never graduated from size 14 children's, much less given birth?

11. Can I refrain from spending the entire class greedily fixating on the enchilada with sour cream I'm going to eat as soon as I'm out of there?

12. Can I refrain from becoming severely depressed as I realize in one hour I have burned off enough calories to offset exactly one stinking bite of jelly doughnut?

13. Can I remember that God loves me for who I am on the inside, and that having thighs that don't clap as I walk may be my goal, but isn't necessarily His?

So you want to sign up for that exercise class? Go ahead. It'll be good for you. But if you're all done with that jelly doughnut, mind if I finish it? I seemed to have worked up quite an appetite just getting into my bra.

Proverbs 31:30 says, "Charm is deceitful and beauty is vain, but a woman who fears the LORD, she shall be praised" (NASB).

Chicken 'n' Dumplings

Becky Freeman

By far the biggest difference between my husband, Scott, and me is this: I have no athletic ability—at all—while Scott is naturally tall and thin, works out with weights, and runs for the sheer pleasure of it. He also stays in shape by building our home, a chronic project that has taken up the better part of the last seven or eight years.

Recently, Scott finished the second story but refused to build a set of stairs to it. When I questioned the wisdom of this decision, he informed me that stairs were for sissies and what he had in mind would constitute a bit of an obstacle course—a splendid opportunity for family fitness and fun. I argued that I liked being a sissy, but alas, to no avail.

Scott, being Chief Builder in charge, created three ways to get from one floor to the other. Choice Number One—mine—is the "lean-to ladder." Choice Number Two—preferred choice for the

kids who literally come swinging into the breakfast room like Tarzan—is "the rope." Choice Number Three is Scott's "rock-climbing wall." Yes, my family is literally climbing the walls.

As one might imagine, I am not exactly a rock climbing kind of woman. I'm not even a jumping jack or jogging kind of gal. I'm short and—let's just say I'm currently reading my 1,789th diet book for the utter euphoria of imagining what I might look like if I ever did get in shape. If reading books about losing weight would somehow do the trick, I'd currently be the size of a coffee stirrer.

A while back, I lunched with three women friends—Linda, Lori, and Mimi. Whatever possessed me to accept an invitation to dine with three women whose combined weight is probably less than that of my salad plate, I'll never know. And predictably the conversation soon turned to weight control. Linda began her pep talk.

"Becky, you've got to start running. I feel so great about myself since I've started jogging—it's unbelievable." Mimi nodded in agreement, "Yes, it's given me a real feeling of power." She paused to flex her beautifully tanned biceps and added, "We are women, hear us roar!"

With so much energy surging in the atmosphere around me, I suddenly had the overpowering urge to take a nap. *I am woman, hear me snore.*

Though Lori, who is about the size of a trim gnat, had been quiet throughout the cheerleading session, I knew she shared my distaste for habitual exercise. And sure enough, when Linda complained that she hated to take off two weeks from her running schedule for a needed surgery, Lori leaned my direction and covered her mouth with her napkin. "I don't know about you," she

whispered softly, "but I'd rather have the surgery." *I can't agree with you more,* I thought.

Regardless of how I feel about exercise and the excessive discussion thereof, it was difficult to argue with the results Linda and Mimi were getting. They were both stunning. *Didn't Scott deserve a thin, athletic, roaring wife too?* I sighed. "This fat has to go!" I declared soon after that ladies' lunch date, and with courageous resolve, I took off running.

On "Day One" my son, Zeke, an athlete like his father, observed my warm-up time with refreshing candor, but I ignored his guffaws and skipped out the door. Somewhere around the bend of the first block, I thought I could hear the theme from *Chariots of Fire* playing in my head.

♥ ♥ ♥ ♥ ♥

The key is to do something so dramatically different to your head that you create a diversion from your well-padded body.

♥ ♥ ♥ ♥ ♥

In little more than a week, I began running triathlons. Well, actually they were more like tri-ath-lawns. I would run past at least three lawns before collapsing. Then as I lay on the asphalt gasping for air, Scott would jog circles around me.

It was fun for a while—both of us being athletes and all. But soon, I headed back to my books, finding it much more stimulating to read about exercise than to really do it.

Besides, I was thrilled to find that there are several practical and viable alternatives to losing weight. One method that works particularly well for me is diversion. This is how it goes: For the past thirty-nine years, I have been a brunette. Last week, however, I decided to try life as a semi-blond and had half of my hair

glitzed in a golden hue. All week long, friends have been stopping me saying, "Something's different—have you lost weight?" See what I mean? For fifty bucks and two hours in a beauty shop, the world thought I'd lost ten pounds. The key is to do something so dramatically different to your head that you create a diversion from your well-padded body.

The second tactic has to do with the power of suggestion. I use this on my husband sometimes with amazing results. It works like this: I put on a dress in a size slightly larger than I normally wear and say, "Scott, would you look how much room there is in this dress?"

With no more prompting than that, he will usually comment, "I'm so proud of you, Honey. I could tell you were losing weight. Good job!" Or even though the scales may be shouting something to the contrary, I say aloud, "I'm feeling kind of thin today, sort of leaner and more energetic." With a knowing nod, Scott will affirm that he, too, has noticed how much I seem to be trimming up.

And finally, the easiest method of pseudo-weight control is camouflage. I recently bought a long dark plaid jumper, which fit well, with a nice wide belt, and paired it with a white, wide collared blouse. It was a size—hey, am I nuts? I'm not telling you that, but I will say it was in the upper teens. I immediately took it home, cut out the size tag and tossed that large number in the trash can. Who needs to know what size our clothes are anyway? If the dress fits, wear it! All I know is the fabric feels nice, and I feel pretty when I wear it. It's one of those outfits with long lines that makes everyone wonder if I've lost weight. I get all the psychological goodies without the stress of a diet—a win-win situation all around.

Club Sweat

Charlene Ann Baumbich

Any day now, George and I are going to take a marvelous trip. I'll be walking every step of the way; he will be rowing.

Oh, the places we'll go, and the toning and strengthening we'll achieve, all in our basement while our bodies work out and our minds ride to healthfulness. You see, we are the proud owners of a rowing machine and a treadmill. Oh, and we also have one of those jumpy things that looks like a round, miniature trampoline, so maybe we'll hop a few miles, too. After all, healthy is good. Svelte is in. And exercise is not only popular, it's something we can do together.

But first we must peruse the possibilities. Master the maneuvers. Tame the technicalities. Delve into discipline. Stop the rhetoric and activate the garden slug that lurks in both of us. Trying to begin an exercise program when you're an old married

couple can boggle the mind. Jump ropes, electronic bicycles, step aerobics, videos…. The staggering options grow by the advertising minute.

Of course, some options can be eliminated if you have children in college or are on a tight budget. The first is expensive health clubs. Not only are there annual fees, but those bright, multi-layered spandex outfits cost bucks, not to mention the cool gym bags and appropriate shoes. And let's face it, no matter how trendy we try to be, we're…not.

Just the other day my only jeans that fit tore right at the bottom of my buttocks and inner thigh. You might be thinking that I'm in style now. After all, teenagers and young adults are paying extra for jeans with fashionable rips. And the grunge look is in. However, trendy folks do not have cellulite oozing through their rips and settling like a wad of silly putty on the chair next to them.

Several years ago I won a year's membership to a weight-training club. I donned my leotards and went once. My trainer explained what I should achieve on the first of several torture machines. Even with zero weight on that first upper-body apparatus, I couldn't bring my arms together. With defeat and humility, I asked if my strong husband could take over my membership. "Nontransferable." George sighed at the news; I don't believe it was the sound of disappointment. Thankfully, my membership expired.

After a recuperation period, we then decided the cheapest option would be to take Wonderdog Butch on a walk every evening. Experts say a twenty-minute walk done regularly is a good place to begin. But no sidewalks, no good weather, and no cooperation from our disobedient, lunging, and entangling mutt

soon dissuaded us from this budding idea, but our gymnastic minds kept flexing for new options.

Shortly thereafter, my grandmother died and left me a small amount of money. "I know, George. I'll get us one of those rowing machines." And so I did. I rowed once and my sciatica screamed at me. Grandma's been gone four years now; that's about how long the rowing machine with the broken roller has sat, untouched, in the corner.

Since we began our quest for fitness, we've heard about lots of "just right" pieces of exercise equipment that now lurk in people's bedroom corners camouflaged by clothing they've flung on the convenient handlebars. Just the other day I clipped a personal ad from the local paper: "Soloflex with attachments $500, Trek 760 with turbo trainer $250," followed by a phone number. Gosh. Attachments, trainers, turbo stuff. Sounds downright painful, doesn't it? I didn't make the call.

Personally, I cannot understand why anyone would want to actually have buns of steel.

But with relentless pursuit, George and I scanned the video counters for just the right exercise program. Many caught his eye. Not because of promised benefits, but because of the "art work" on the boxes. Personally, I cannot understand why anyone would want to actually have buns of steel. Buns of *steel*? Can you imagine plopping down at your desk and hearing a sound reminiscent of The Gong Show? You'd probably shatter your teeth.

And so we purchased two Richard Simmons' exercise videos. I used them sweating to the oldies on more than one occasion. But

after actually viewing the tapes, Big George decided he just wasn't ready to clap those hands and jive; he decided to fix the rowing machine instead.

Meanwhile, my stress level (partly induced by the guilt caused by all the exercise we weren't getting) was calibrating at the high end of the scale. Since exercise is a known stress defuser, it was time to stop dawdling and just do it. Walking still seemed the least taxing on the body; treadmill talk began; shopping followed; the treadmill arrived. George said I should figure it out and then tell him how to use it. Seemed like a good idea to me.

Lesson number one: Never use new exercise equipment when you're home alone, especially if it's electronic. By the time I finished reading the directions, I was exhausted. Straddle the belt. Attach heart monitor to ear. Determine miles-per-hour and all other settings. Attach safety shut-off to clothing. (I should have paid more attention to this last one.)

I hurled myself off the conveyor belt on more than one occasion. After I told George about my adventures, he wanted to install a floor-height phone next to the treadmill so we could call 911 from the splat position. Like the little trooper my dad raised me to be, however, I climbed back on that bronco and now have tamed it, although I don't ride often enough.

George and I are once again in the "we're-not-kidding" planning stages of exercising together. And we're *not kidding.* We're already burning calories by flapping our jaws talking about the great and wondrous journeys we plan to take. He will row; I will walk. Perhaps a few tunes in the background will enhance our healthy togetherness and create an enchanted atmosphere for our thrice-weekly departure.

Others can talk about their need to stop by the club or their latest aerobic class. But as for me and my honey, we're gonna travel. By hook or by crook, we're gonna conquer this exercise thing together. And although we may not end up with buns of steel, we have high hopes that our rewards will at least produce bellies of laughter and years of health.

4

making humor
your hobby

A Running Start

You know you're getting old when you need a running start to go for a walk.

—Martha Bolton,
Didn't My Skin Used to Fit?

Time to Unravel a
Sweater Mystery

Marti Attoun

I like wool, but I've never trusted it. The minute I invest in a lovely wool sweater, it starts shrinking.

Before I can say "where's the receipt?" it's shriveled and barely covers the shoulders of a two-liter soda bottle.

But lately, I've battled a knottier problem: the case of the incredibly growing sweater.

The moss-colored sweater fit my husband perfectly last year. The pullover summered on a hanger in the closet until two weeks ago when my husband pulled it on for work.

Suddenly, the sleeves looked really long—orangutan-long.

"What's happening here?" he sputtered. The shoulders on the woven ramie wonder had dropped a good three inches. The hip-fitting bottom had slipped, too.

I tried to be optimistic because he was already late for work.

"At least you won't need gloves," I told him. "Just bunch it up around the waist, tuck under the sleeves and try not to move around too much. No one will notice."

"What? That I'm drowning in a sweater?" he shouted.

I don't know where "ramie" comes from—plant, animal or Afghanistan—but it's one evil-doing fiber.

By noon, according to my husband's account, the sweater was moving in a southerly direction at the rate of an inch an hour. By midafternoon, his mid was so bunched up it looked like he was wearing a personal floatation device.

By the time he swaddled in that evening, the sweater groped his knees. It was twice the sweater we'd bought.

"My word, take that thing off. It's spreading faster than kudzu," I told him.

By noon, the sweater was moving in a southerly direction at the rate of an inch an hour.

I tied it up in a garbage bag and hauled it to Mom the next day to donate to the mission barrel.

"Why, that's too good a sweater to give to the poor," she said. My mother's motto is "waste not, want not." She insisted on washing the sweater in hot water and reshaping it.

I was skeptical, but Mom has rescued the family's wardrobe many times, using hand-me-down toxic formulas to scare stains out of shirts and duct tape to rip lint from corduroys.

By afternoon, she'd wrestled the ramie back down to a "medium" and had it blocked out and drying on towels on the kitchen table.

Thinking it might go to XL again on a hanger, I neatly folded the sweater in a drawer. Yesterday, my husband was desperate for something to wear and decided to give the sweater one more chance.

"Your mother is sure that the sweater isn't going to spread out again?" he asked, still suffering from sweater shock.

"She stabilized it," I assured him.

As he walked out the door, I swear I saw that ramie relax and descend a notch, but I held my tongue.

The only way to unravel this mystery is with a pair of scissors. Tomorrow, I'm taking Mom a big bag of fluffy moss-colored yarn. I'm sure she can find a use for it.

How to Break All the Rules (and Still Throw a Great Party)

Lynn Bowen Walker

Giving a party used to mean pulling out all the stops, primping and preening not only ourselves but also our homes till we were so unrecognizable that those around us wondered if the real family was tied up in a closet somewhere.

Thankfully, those days are over. We're in the new millennium now, where party-giving, like hairdos and exercise regimens, has become much more relaxed. Here, then, are the rules as they used to be, and today's new improved version.

Old Rule Number 1: Before throwing a party, pull out the Julia Child classic French cuisine cookbook and immerse yourself in terms like "creme fraiche" and "ragout." Begin early as it will take you the better part of a week just to find the Julia Child classic French cuisine cookbook.

New Rule Number 1: Keep cooking to a minimum. If, when

invited, a guest should happen to exclaim, "What can I bring?" practice casually answering, "How about boeuf bourguignon?"

Old Rule Number 2: Scrub your house with Brillo pads until your fingers bleed. Make your house look like nobody really lives there.

New Rule Number 2: Shove all the clutter under the beds. Dim the lights and get out candles. Plan to play lots of blindfold games.

Old Rule Number 3: The day before the party, spend 95 minutes painting chocolate onto leaves to use as a dessert garnish. Hide painted chocolate leaves from friend who thinks Martha Stewart should be shot.

New Rule Number 3: Low-key is o-kay. You don't have to serve food from cute little carved-out cucumber canoes. Paper plates are fine. Mismatched dishes are fine. Cups shaped like Shrek's head are fine.

Old Rule Number 4: Give your family a crash course in good manners. Instruct them to ask for food to be passed rather than lunging for it. Pretend your kids always use a knife and fork.

New Rule Number 4: Borrow your sister's well-behaved family for the occasion. If anyone asks if those are really your children, lie.

Old Rule Number 5: Watch in horror as, three minutes before your guests arrive, your husband begins to simultaneously clean ashes from the fireplace, replace the window that's been broken since 1992, and stain the redwood deck. (TIP: Practice smiling through clenched teeth.)

New Rule Number 5: Do not tell your husband you are even having a party. As the first guests arrive, murmur, "Oh honey, look! It's Charlie and Laura! Good thing I made that roast this morning!"

Old Rule Number 6: In consideration of guests who never

travel without their fat gram wall murals, serve steamed vegetables and sliced tofu. Hand each guest a pair of chopsticks. Excuse yourself to the bathroom to sneak a Snickers.

New Rule Number 6: Drop the charade. Admit you sometimes feed your family Pop Tarts and call it dinner. Serve chocolate chip cookies for appetizers. Like the bumper sticker says, "Eat dessert first. Life is uncertain."

Old Rule Number 7: Artfully arrange fresh flowers into a tasteful centerpiece.

New Rule Number 7: Who has time for artful arrangements? Gather the clutter on your kitchen table, sweep it into a pile, and insert a mini American flag. Claim it's the country-kitchen look.

Old Rule Number 8: Orchestrate the evening as you would a well-conducted symphony. Bring orchid-raising Uncle Lester over to meet your neighbor who nurses tropical fish back to health. Pretend they have something in common. If after-dinner conversation lags, shepherd everyone into another room where they can politely ditch the bore you seated them next to at dinner.

New Rule Number 8: Don't count on adult conversation to carry the evening. Witty repartee may run out before the taco chips do. Hang spoons from your noses. Hand each guest a paper party hat. Take your husband into the spare bedroom, shut the door, and secretly laugh at guests wearing dorky paper hats.

Old Rule Number 9: When it's time for guests to leave, help them find their coats, escort them to the door, and warmly thank them for coming.

New Rule Number 9: Remind your guests that you have video footage of them with spoons hanging from their noses. Suggest it is *their* turn to host the next party.

Family Antiques Expert

Marti Attoun

I don't need the experts from the "Antiques Roadshow" to tell me whether I've unearthed a $50,000 pickle jar or a 59-cent Milk of Magnesia bottle. My brother-in-law Dan has acquired a reputation as the family "antiques expert."

Every family has one of these—someone who "knows something about antiques." I'm not sure how Dan acquired his title, other than he's lived a long time and has a jeweler's loupe. At any rate, his opinion is free, which is as low-dollar as you can get, and he usually only laughs for an hour after inspecting one of my finds.

On a recent junk-sale junket, I lugged home a two-level brown crockery thing. The vintage owner had used it as a doorstop for 30 years, as had her mother. This was a dead give-away to me that I had something valuable. The minute you slap

the word "estate" on an object, it adds a heap of cachet and at least 50 percent to its value.

"I only paid a buck for this wonderful old strawberry pot," I bragged to my husband.

He looked it over. "That's too shallow to be a strawberry planter," he informed me. "Looks like some kind of light, probably an old transformer."

I pounced on eBay and checked out all the transformers at auction. Not one resembled my 15-pounder, which was growing more rare by the moment. I inspected it with a magnifying glass. Naturally, it was unmarked, except by filth. I didn't dare clean it and damage its patina.

"I'm heading out to Dan's," I told my husband as I swaddled my precious crockery in bubble wrap and a box.

I settled the treasure in the middle of Dan's kitchen table as gently as if it were a jeweled Fabergé egg.

I settled the treasure in the middle of Dan's kitchen table as gently as if it were a jeweled Fabergé egg. And then I unwrapped it.

"Why in the world are you hauling around a dirty old chicken feeder?" he asked.

I didn't have an intelligent answer. "I thought you might want to use it for a porch light," didn't sound too bright.

"Oh, you know, I just wanted to see if it's worth anything," I told him.

"It's worth a lot if you're a hungry chicken," he said.

This is why it pays to have an antiques expert in the family, so you don't embarrass yourself in front of strangers.

Dan has rescued me several times since I decided to supplement my freelancing career with flea-lancing. He still keeps one of my 25-cent "finds" on display for when he needs a 10 dollar laugh. I felt confident when I tagged the "vintage ramrod." After all, I'd seen old muzzle-loading rifles before with their skinny metal rods. This old ramrod would be a steal at 10 bucks.

Fortunately, Dan spied the tagged treasure before it went into my booth.

"So," he asked me, "where's the rest of your umbrella?"

I'd paid a quarter for one spoke of an umbrella.

I'd like to say that I've gotten smarter, but I don't want to overvalue my merchandise. Let's just say that I'm developing quite a thick patina.

queen of
domesticity

Apron Inspirations

My mom always wore an apron when she was preparing meals. I'd carry on the tradition and wear an apron today, but my family is concerned it might inspire me to cook.

—PATSY CLAIRMONT,
SPORTIN' A 'TUDE

Vanamaniacs: Mom's Checklist to Know When to Clean Out the Van

Kathi Hunter

- When one of your carpool kids says he left his replica of the White House built out of Popsicle sticks at home— and you remember you have one in the trunk.

- Your dog refuses to go for a ride.

- You seriously wonder if you need to cook dinner tonight—maybe the kids could just dig between the seats for French fries.

- Your teenager, the one whose room looks like a possible location for the next Survivor, takes one look inside the van and says, "That's OK, I'll walk to the mall."

- With the assortment of sweatshirts, team jerseys, hats, and socks in the backseat, you could dress the entire Brady Bunch—including Alice.

- You wait the extra month to get the factory ordered "Desert Sand" upholstery for your van (knowing it's the only color that doesn't show Diet Coke spills).

- The most common phrase heard from the backseat is "Oh…that's where it is."

- You find McDonald's toys from The Little Mermaid, Beauty and the Beast, and The Lion King under the seats.

- You decide to give your pregnant sister the baby's car seat that is still strapped into the back of your van (the baby now has pimples and a date on Friday night).

- Your kids, peering into your Starbuck's mug squeal, "Cool, can we bring that to science class?"

Keeping the Home Fires Burning

Susan Duke

"Honey, can you come home," I sobbed on the phone to my husband. "Now?"

"What's wrong?" Harvey asked with deep concern.

"I kind of caught the kitchen on fire!" I wailed.

When he arrived on the scene, he was relieved to find less damage than my trembling voice had portrayed. After working a few hours in my home office, I'd gone into the kitchen to cook some bacon for a sandwich. The portable phone (which normally rests on a base in the kitchen) rang in the living room.

In the seconds it took to answer the phone, I smelled smoke. I ran back into the kitchen just as my stove, vent-a-hood, and wooden cabinets burst into flames. By the time I reached the stove, the fire had extinguished itself.

It turned out to be one of those all-things-work-together-for-good situations. Our insurance man determined that the smoke

damage warranted replacing the cabinets, our fifteen-year-old stove, and outdated dishwasher. I wouldn't exactly recommend this sort of home remodeling, but I accepted it as a merciful blessing.

I wouldn't exactly recommend this sort of home remodeling, but I accepted it as a merciful blessing.

Whenever we travel down memory lane, Harvey reminds me of another kitchen disaster we survived one Saturday afternoon when I whipped up our family's favorite dessert—pineapple upside-down cake. When the timer rang, I carefully removed the long, glass, baking pan from the oven and set it on the stovetop to cool. It smelled scrumptious. Waiting in the family room, we counted the moments before our cake was cool enough to serve.

That's when we heard the explosion.

"What's that?" Harvey asked, rushing to the kitchen. "Oh no! Oh no!" he groaned.

The cake had blown up! Unknowingly, I'd set the dish on a burner that was turned on low. The Pyrex dish shattered—embedding cake and glass in a gazillion pieces all over the walls, ceiling, floor, and countertops.

Thankfully, Harvey is great at cleaning *and* cooking. I recently bought him a little sign that hangs by our new stove: "Real Men Wear Aprons, Buddy." He loves it—and says I've proven that a woman's place is not necessarily in the kitchen—but there are plenty of other ways to keep the home fires burning.

The Sunday Morning Comics (and Other Indispensable Gardening Tools)

Karen Scalf Linamen

Two days ago a woman said to me, "I'd love to see your garden sometime."

Sara has never been to my home, but she read about my gardening efforts in my book *Just Hand Over the Chocolate and No One Will Get Hurt.*

In the book I painted vivid pictures of daylilies and hollyhocks, morning glories and hydrangeas. I described hours spent puttering in the dirt with my kids, playing with caterpillars and watering cans.

I smiled lamely at Sara. "Oh," I said. "The Garden."

My garden was once as beautiful as I described. But if Sara came to my house today she would find one neglected bed of pansies, an overgrown trellis of Lady Banksia roses, and some diehard lamb's ears.

Not to mention weeds.

You see, last summer I was feeling sort of overwhelmed and found myself trying to simplify my life. It was while in this state of mind that I thought about the amount of water it was going to take to keep my garden thriving through the scorching Texas summer. Somehow, I came to the conclusion I could save time and money by letting my garden succumb to the heat and simply purchasing all new plants in the spring.

So now it's April, and I'm thinking I should just go down to the bank and take out a second mortgage on my home. Or add Home Depot to the signature card on my checking account. Or sell my children to the gypsies. After all, replenishing all my beds with blooms isn't going to go easy on my wallet. In fact, I suspect the National Debt will seem quite manageable in comparison.

Not to mention the labor it's going to require.

But when it comes to reclaiming the yard, at least I got a good start yesterday: I made my fourteen-year-old mow the lawn.

Those of you with teenagers realize this is no small accomplishment. I figure I could have reseeded the lawn, put in a vegetable garden, and built a wooden deck with the amount of energy it took to prod, threaten, and cajole my teen into finishing the task at hand. Which begs the question: Why is it that a teen who can't hear a mother's instructions at three paces can hear the ring of the kitchen phone twenty yards away over the drone of one lawnmower and a headset blaring "Collide" by Jars of Clay?

Of course, my teen is easier to motivate when the riding mower is working (I think she pretends it's an SUV). But ever since the riding mower conked out and she's been stuck with the

gas-powered push model, getting an hour's labor out of her requires nothing short of a cattle prod and an act of Congress.

But the gardening device I'm really anxious to try is my mini-tiller. I bought it last fall and have yet to break ground with it. According to the glowing advertising claims that prompted me to part with an amount of money that could have fed and clothed a third-world country for the better part of a year, this machine not only tills, weeds, aerates, mulches, trims, and edges, it should give me thinner thighs and whiter teeth as well.

What the company neglected to tell me was that my 400-horsepower weed-busting Garden Genie would be delivered to me, ready-to-be-assembled, in a shoebox.

I've seen head lice larger than the hundreds of parts I'm supposed to be able to assemble into a gasoline-driven workhorse in only 1,047 easy steps.

In hindsight, taking the potting soil out of the plastic bags might not have been a bad idea either.

Which is why the Garden Genie is still in its shoebox, and last week my daughters and I prepared our first flower bed of the season by throwing layers of newspaper down on the weeds and then covering them up with four bags of potting soil. (The downside is that I'll have to plant flowers with very shallow root systems, at least until the newspaper finishes killing the weeds and then decomposes. In hindsight, taking the potting soil out of the plastic bags might not have been a bad idea either.)

You know, gardening can be enjoyable labor.

Or it can feel frustrating and even futile.

A lot depends on whether or not you've got the right tools.

Resources like the right mower, handy tiller, and adequate water can make a world of difference when you're in the process of nurturing tender growing things.

Cultivating soil with a weedwacker, for example, is a recipe for disaster. Cutting grass with cuticle scissors is a one-way ticket to the Funny Farm. And planting bulbs with a kitchen spoon not only takes twice as long but can make your coffee taste kind of earthy the next morning.

I understand these principles when it comes to organic growth (just don't ask me how I knew about the earthy coffee).

So why do I forget they apply to spiritual growth as well?

I want to grow, thrive, bloom, and bear fruit spiritually. But am I equipping myself with the right tools? Or am I trying to do the job armed with a teaspoon and the Sunday funnies?

What are the power tools of spiritual growth? This list isn't definitive, but I've got a few ideas: Prayer. Fasting. The Word of God. Praise and worship. Accountability to godly friends. Confession. Bible study. Spending time in the presence of God.

I don't know about you, but some days I think my backyard is a tropical paradise compared to my spiritual landscaping.

Spring is a great time to spruce up the yard. But maybe it's a good reminder to tend to my soul as well.

I was going to spend the afternoon potting a few patio plants. But before I head outdoors, I think I'll spend an hour in my favorite armchair with my Bible and a cup of coffee. It should be a rewarding time.

Even if my coffee does taste like dirt.

6

looking fine, feeling foolish

Costly Comparisons

My self-image would be fine if there weren't so many other people around to compare myself to.

—C. McNair Wilson,
Everyone Wants to Go to Heaven, but...

Say Good-bye to Good Intentions

Karen Scalf Linamen

I finally did it.

I thumbed through the phone book, found the number, dialed it, and made an appointment for two weeks from today.

I'm going to see an electrologist.

I've been meaning to make an appointment for months. Lots of months. Actually, dozens of them. But can you blame me for procrastinating?

You've heard of electrolysis, right? It's a way of getting rid of unwanted hair on your face and body. The way I understand it, I'm paying about a dollar a minute to have a certified technician stick a miniature cattle prod into my hair follicles, then turn to a hunchbacked assistant and shout the words, "Throw the switch!"

I think it also has to be a stormy night.

It's a drastic measure, I know. But you'll have to trust me when I say that I'm not taking this step lightly. I can either submit to

these Mary-Shelleyesque electrical treatments, or I can continue resembling Wolfman Jack. It's come down to this.

Actually, I've been battling these two dozen annoying chin hairs for several years now. The final straw occurred this past weekend. We had friends coming over Sunday afternoon to watch a Cowboys game on TV, and I was in the bathroom getting ready, and...well...I nicked myself shaving.

Not my leg, mind you. My face.

I stemmed the bleeding with a twist of toilet paper and looked at myself in the mirror. I thought, this is what happens to fourteen-year-old boys who borrow their dad's razor for the first time. They look just like this, with toilet paper spit wads on their chins. Of course, fourteen-year-old boys don't wear Caffe Latte lipstick by Estee Lauder, but other than that, the similarities were striking.

It was time to take permanent action.

Even though I haven't had my appointment yet, it feels good to have made the call. There's something about finally getting around to a long-intended project that feels really great.

In fact, I'm so inspired by how good I feel right now that I'm wondering what other loose-end projects I can tackle. What else have I been putting off that I could get out of the way?

Oh. I just remembered one. Okay, I'll admit this one's no fun. In fact, having my follicles electrocuted by a mad scientist ranks higher on my list of favorite activities than this next project.

You probably know what I'm thinking about. In fact, my guess is that you're overdue as well.

I'm thinking about The Dreaded Well-Woman Exam.

Who came up with this process, anyway? I mean, a total stranger tells me to wear nothing but a paper towel, plant my feet

in metal stirrups that feel like they've been stored in the freezer, and then I'm supposed to relax and chitchat while he maneuvers a Buick around in there? I don't THINK so.

Sigh.

But it's a necessary evil. I'm going to stop procrastinating and make the call. You should too.

Let's see. What else have I been intending to do? I'm going to make it something fun this time. Oh, I know! Have lunch with Jeffie Burns. She's the Children's Ministry Director at my church, and she's got a wit sharper than an electrolysis needle. Time spent with Jeffie always gets me laughing and leaves me uplifted. We've been promising to "do lunch" for months. I think I'll nail something down.

January seems to be the month for grandiose new schemes and resolutions. But you know what? I'd love to spend it just catching up on old plans and good intentions.

Something else I've always intended to do has been to read through the Bible in a year. In fact, one of the Bibles I have is already divided into 365 readings. I've just never cracked the cover. I'd have to do a little catch-up here at the beginning, but I know it would be an enjoyable journey.

You know, good intentions and a buck'll buy you a cup of coffee. Maybe it's time to turn some of those good intentions into reality.

Wanna join me? Call your OB-GYN. Have lunch with a friend. Dust off your Bible.

And if you've been battling unwanted hairs, take heart. I hear Dr. Frankenstein's available for evening and weekend appointments as well.

Celebrating the Unexpected!

Sue Buchanan

Not everyone is keen on surprises, and sometimes there are reasons why! I'll never forget going to a birthday party once where the guest of honor had been told by her husband, while they were walking up their front walk after work, to hurry and change clothes and he would take her to a special place for her birthday. Little did she know that we, her friends, were waiting in the living room to surprise her. Also little did anyone know that as she walked up the steps to their second-floor apartment, she was unbuttoning her blouse, or that at the exact moment she would be entering the room, she would be flinging her blouse in the air. It was more surprise than *any one* of us bargained for!

Whether or not you like surprises, let's face it, life is full of them, and perhaps it's best to sit back, and if at all possible,

enjoy them. Sometimes you work toward some goal for months on end, and everything goes wrong. But what God has in store is far beyond what we could think or dream. *His surprises are the best of all!*

It was more surprise than any one of us bargained for!

Only My UPS Man
Knows for Sure

Susan Duke

It was one of those bright, sunny, near-perfect days in May. My energy level was charged, and I was in the mood to do some serious housecleaning. *While I work,* I thought, *I'll try out my new green herbal facial mask and condition my hair.*

Once I applied the green goop and placed my bright red shower cap over my conditioner-lathered hair, I was set. I cranked up the stereo with some lively soulful music, opened the doors and windows, grabbed a mop, pail, dust rag, and furniture polish, and started cleaning to the music.

I never heard the UPS truck pull into my driveway—but as I twirled and danced through the kitchen, I stopped in my tracks at the sight of my brown-uniformed friend standing in the doorway. I ran to turn down the music and hurried back to the door.

"I'm sorry, I never heard you drive up," I said nonchalantly.

"I can see that, Ma'am," he offered, grinning broadly. "I have several items on the truck for you," he said, setting the first box on the porch.

Within minutes the faithful deliveryman had unloaded three huge towsacks (burlap sacks) and five more boxes. On the outside of two boxes were cassette-tape covers with my picture and name on them. Two other boxes, stamped with my name on the outside, contained books. And the last box was labeled...*Caution: Flammable Contents.*

Once I applied the green goop and placed my bright red shower cap over my conditioner-lathered hair, I was set.

"Quite a variety here today, Ma'am. I've never delivered towsacks to anyone. I thought you might be a singer, because I've brought tapes to you before, but I have to admit, sometimes I wonder, Ma'am...just what all *do* you do?"

Suddenly, I caught a glimpse of my crackled green face in my sparkling glass door. "Well, I'm sure you'd never guess from today's appearance, but I'm a speaker, writer, and singer. And I make my own potpourri. The towsacks contain wood shavings and the 'flammable' box contains essential oils."

"Are you a clown too?" he chuckled, staring at my mud-dried face.

"No," I snickered, "just trying to get beautiful."

We are often labeled and defined by what we do. But God showed me something that day. We are not our labels. Speaking is not who I am. Neither is writing, or singing, or potpourri-making. These things are only a part of the sum total—green face and all, of the woman God created me to be.

7

clutter bugs unite!

A Child's Prayer

Dear God,

Do you get your angels to do all the work? Mommy says we are her angels, and we have to do everything.

Love, Maria

—PHIL CALLAWAY,
WHO PUT THE SKUNK IN THE TRUNK?

Checks and Unbalances

Martha Bolton

Few people overdraw their checking accounts deliberately. Usually it's due to a simple error in addition or subtraction, a deposit they credited more than once, or the 14 missing checks they forgot to enter into their checkbook.

Still, when it does happen, it can be quite embarrassing. Once while trying to cash a check in the drive-up lane at my bank, the teller repossessed my tube, then announced over the PA (and local radio stations) that I was overdrawn. As she passed my check back to me through the three cars on my left, I thought to myself, how could I, a person who keeps impeccable records on the backs of grocery store receipts, be overdrawn?

My first reaction was to argue the fact, but since she had disconnected my microphone, I decided to take my problem inside.

I was sure it had to be a computer error, so while waiting in line inside the bank, I went over my figures again. And again. And

again. But I kept coming up with the same answer: the crayola scribbling in my checkbook correctly indicated a $300 balance.

When my turn finally came, I walked over to the teller and explained my problem. She listened graciously, then sent me to another teller who listened graciously before sending me to another teller.

"Can you help me?" I pleaded, handing her my checkbook. "I'm overdrawn and I don't understand why. According to my records, I should still have $300 in my account."

She carefully thumbed through my register.

"You call these records?" she snapped. "Your check numbers aren't even in order."

"Of course not," I explained emphatically. "I don't write them in order, why should I enter them in order?"

She didn't laugh.

"I don't write them in order, why should I enter them in order?"

"And who was this check written to?" she asked, pointing to the blank line at check number 541.

"I thought you'd know," I smiled.

Again, she didn't laugh. I quickly added, "Look, whenever I can't remember who a check was written to, I merely deduct $25.00 from my balance until I receive my monthly statement. If I find out it was for more, I adjust my balance accordingly."

Unimpressed, she merely walked over to the cancelled-checks file and returned waving the check in question.

"Check number 541 was your house payment," she said dryly.

I remained calm.

"That still shouldn't have mattered," I said, "because I'm sure I've overpaid on enough other missing checks to absorb most of the difference."

She lowered her head, sighed, then continued her review.

"Ah-ha," she exclaimed. "I see here that check number 513 was for $86.18 but you only entered $42.18 in your checkbook."

"Oh, that. That was for our marital savings."

"A joint savings account?"

"No. I mean to save our marriage. You see, I bought a new dress at Penney's for $86.18, but only entered $42.18 in the register. I hid the other $44.00 in check number 516, which was actually written for $17.00, but I listed it as $61.00 so no one would know check number 513 was actually for $44.00 more."

"Don't you realize that bookkeeping like that won't get you anywhere?" she snapped.

"We've been married for almost 20 years."

"Well, what about your service charges," she continued. "It appears you've never entered your monthly service charges."

"I figured you'd say something if you weren't getting paid. And anyway, I still have my cushion."

"Your cushion?"

"Yes," I replied, confidently. "My June 10 deposit. I never entered it into my register."

"Why not?"

"I like to think I have less money in the bank than I really do. It helps me budget."

"But how do you balance your account at the end of each month?" she asked, slamming my checkbook shut and shoving it back to me.

"I've never HAD to balance it until today!" I grumbled.

"Look," she said. "Our records indicate you're overdrawn $45.00. We'll have to go by those figures until you can prove an error on our part. Now, will you be making a deposit or not?"

I hung my head in despair. It was no use. This hard-line teller was going to believe a lousy computer over *my* records.

"I guess so," I sighed, then added meekly, "Will you take a check?"

…Oh, well. At least we never have to worry about God's love coming up short.

It May Be Chaos, but It's Mine

Charlene Ann Baumbich

Every woman likes to have Her Space. I, however, seem to need My Space Here and My Space There. I even seem to need My Space in Your Space on hormone-rushing days.

One of the spaces I occupy most often is my ten-by-ten office. It's disorganized, dusty, it's dripping with signs and photos and papers papers papers. It houses my ink well collection, a piece of bark with words made out of macaroni, a piece of art that Bret made in day camp eons ago. Beside it, a plaque that says "Never try to teach a pig to sing. It wastes your time and annoys the pig." It has necessities such as a clock and a thingie that when you blow into it, makes that obnoxious raspberry sound. I blow it often because that's how I'm feeling. Other musical instruments include a harmonica I want to learn to play and the mouthpiece to a saxophone I'd like to buy one day. And learn how to play. And candles, of course, and on and on and I love it.

I love this space, except on days when I'm tripping over all my stuff, and then I think I need to move My Space to a bigger space. I tell George, "I just need more space to organize my stuff," but we both know that would never really happen.

I have actually cleaned my office space a few times. I mean *really* cleaned it. As opposed to the times when I just stack things up and give it a quick wipe. But more typically, my office is where I throw everything when company comes because I can close the door. There's no reason for anyone to see my office (unless they're snooping around upstairs when they use the bathroom, in which case they *deserve* to see the mess.)

"Don't go up there! It annoys the pig." Of course, they probably wouldn't be upstairs in the bathroom because we have a downstairs bath. No matter how I time it, I'm always running late, and it's always the upstairs bathroom I don't get to before company arrives. So, when someone heads that way, I yell, as their foot is midway up step two, "No! Use the one down here!"

This is when I unknowingly infringe upon George's space; the space in his brain where he logs items that store up before exploding. One day when we were grumbling about something unrelated to cleaning, George delivered a punch below the belt. He hollered, I mean he *hollered*, "And after 25 years, what do you think people think is *in* that upstairs bathroom!" I have no answer to that, but obviously, I know something George doesn't know: Every household has its room(s) that doesn't get entered when company comes. Right?

Recently, however, we had a doubly-whammy experience: four three-day overnight guests. Every available space (and espe-

cially My Space and My Hidden Space) would need to be utilized. One of the single young men would have to sleep in my office on a chair that unfolds into a bed; obviously six people would need both bathrooms.

The Good Book says all our days are numbered. Getting my office ready for someone to sleep in it (a tall someone who could see the top shelves when standing and the low ones when sleeping) removed three days from the space of my life.

That was three weeks ago. You should see my office space now.

I mean, "Don't go up there! It annoys the pig."

Clutter Management 101

Karen Scalf Linamen

I'm getting the urge again.

It hits me every year. Maybe it's brought on from thumbing through Target ads and seeing all the plastic storage boxes and closet dividers on sale.

But whatever the reason, every January I get this urge to organize my home.

Some years, I'll admit, I take two aspirin and watch reruns of *Sanford and Son* until The Urge goes away (I suspect this is because, compared to their home, mine looks like it belongs between the covers of *Better Homes and Gardens*).

But other years I get really motivated and make an effort to tame the jungle of clutter in my home.

Of course, this is easier said than done. Sometimes I get the feeling my house is a little like the Eagles' Hotel California: Things check in but they don't check out. (Or is that the Roach

Motel? I can never remember!) What kinds of things? How about clothes that haven't been in style since I had to have my pet rock put to sleep, or my collection of Barry Manilow songs—on eight track—or the two dozen plaques I own that try to assure me that "A Messy Desk Is the Sign of a Creative Mind" (all gifts from friends who know me a little too well).

The only good thing about clutter is that, indeed, one woman's junk is another woman's treasure. One month I managed to clean out two closets and hold a garage sale. I made $400. (I figured if I clean out the rest of my closets I can probably put one of my children through college.)

I'm not sure where all the clutter comes from. Oh sure, junk mail is a big chunk of it. Happy Meal toys comprise another large portion. Half-used tubes of abandoned makeup and facial-care products are another hefty category. And what about those wire hangers? Have you ever once in your life actually purchased a wire hanger? Me neither, I always buy the plastic tube hangers.

So why, even as we speak, are my closets being held hostage by legions of hostile wire hangers?

I have this theory. I have a theory that while my house looks, on the outside, like a perfectly normal single-family dwelling, there are, in reality, sinister forces at work here. I have reason to believe that my house has been hexed and, as a result, any family who lives within these walls will be force to contend with the Curse of the Copulating Clutter.

I know this sounds far-fetched, but I don't know quite how else to explain the fact that every morning I wake to twice as much clutter as the night before. The stuff breeds during the midnight hours, I'm certain of it.

What clutter-management techniques have I acquired? Well,

sometimes, I try to recycle. Over the holidays, for example, I enlisted the artistic talents of friend Gavin Jones to craft a wire metal hanger into a hat from which a sprig of mistletoe could be hung four inches above the head of the wearer.

But we were lucky. Not every unwanted household item can be recycled into something quite so useful.

Think of all the useful things MacGyver could invent from the clutter in my home.

Which gives me an idea. I've always had a crush on Richard Dean Anderson in his role as MacGyver. I'm thinking they should produce a reunion show, and tape it at my house. Think of all the useful things MacGyver could invent from the clutter in my home. Why, put him in one room alone, and he could build a space shuttle. Or a minivan. Or best yet, something I could REALLY put to good use, like Rosie, the robotic maid from the Jetsons.

But the tangible clutter in my home isn't the worst of it. Old magazines, mugs featuring pictures of state capitols, a tray of bobbins belonging to the sewing machine I gave to Goodwill seven years ago—these things may be annoying, but they're manageable.

It's the other clutter in my life that I can't quite get a handle on, the stuff even MacGyver can't touch. Stuff like bad habits and old hurts and painful memories, not to mention lingering lusts and dusty grudges and broken dreams.

Stuff I should have gotten rid of a long time ago.

Maybe I should forget Anderson's Hollywood agents and put in a call to Someone who can REALLY help. There is, after all, a Master Recycler, someone who promises that he can take ALL

things in my life and make them work out—somehow, if I let him—for good. His awesome lemons-into-lemonade abilities even prompted one Bible hero, Joseph, to look into the eyes of the brothers who betrayed him and admit, "What you meant for evil, God meant for good."

God doesn't recycle overnight. Sometimes he takes years. But I'm realizing that he can't even get started on my clutter until I unclench my fists and hand it over.

What he'll make of it all is up to him.

I know it's not very spiritual, but I'll go ahead and say it anyway:

I'm hoping for at least one Rosie out of the whole mess.

8

laughter for the chronologically challenged

The First to Go

They say the mind is the first thing to go...at least, I think that's what they say.

—LAURA JENSEN WALKER,
MENTALPAUSE...AND OTHER MIDLIFE LAUGHS

Betty's Mother

Patricia Wilson

Most of the time, I don't notice that I'm growing older. In some far recess of my mind, my biological clock seems to have stopped at thirty-three years. My mental self-image has no gray in her hair, the wrinkles haven't taken hold, and her chin is still singular.

Occasionally, I catch a glimpse of a much older woman in the bathroom mirror, but I just put that down to bad lighting. When I meet the parents of my children's friends, I am always surprised at how old they look. "Must have started late," I tell myself, ignoring the fact that I was a late-blooming parent myself. And if the policeman who stops my car at the road check seems young enough to be my son, I just assume he's a new recruit.

All in all, I feel that I have my aging process pretty well under control.

Until, that is, I met Betty again. Betty and I had attended elementary school together and high school after that. Even when

we parted to go our separate ways—she to teachers' college and I to a technical school—we still kept in touch. Then we moved on to our own lives and careers. Briefly, we met again when I was a bridesmaid at her wedding, and several months later she came to mine. We didn't meet again for over twenty years, although we did occasionally exchange notes and change-of-address cards.

Through the usual kind of corporate moves, she and her family ended up in Ottawa. To our mutual delight, I was now living a scant hour's drive away. We had never been physically closer. A reunion was in order.

We agreed to meet on our own first, before we brought our families together. It seemed fairer to get all of our "Do you remembers…" out of the way. Neither of us felt we had to wear a rose in our lapel to distinguish us from the crowd. We'd know each other anywhere!

When I arrived, I asked the maître d' whether Mrs. St. Onge was there yet. She wasn't. I settled back to wait.

Then, Betty's mother came through the door! Well, it wasn't Betty's mother…it was Betty. Somehow, I hadn't expected her to look a bit different from my old school friend. I certainly hadn't expected her to look—how can I put it delicately?—middle-aged!

After all, I hadn't changed. Why should she? Then I saw Betty staring at me in the same open-mouthed surprise. Could it be that I now looked like my mother? Impossible! Could it be that I was also middle-aged? Unthinkable!

Betty and I easily picked up where we had left off twenty years earlier. Only now, we were both aware of the richness and full-ness of our lives…lives that had been through joys and sorrows; lives that had experienced grief and pain, happiness and content-

ment, peace and hope and faith. We were so much *more* of what we had been in our youth. Looking back, those girls were mere shadows of the women we had become.

And when we joked about being middle-aged, it was with a wild sense of anticipation: only halfway through and so much more living to be done. Suddenly, I didn't mind those few gray hairs, the extra inches on my middle, the soft chinline, the laughter lines around my eyes. They were my badges of honor, the proof that I had *lived* my life fully.

Could it be that I now looked like my mother? Impossible!

I don't really like growing older, mind you. I don't like being told by a doctor who is still wearing braces on his teeth, "You're not getting any younger, you know," and I don't like having to remember to take my vitamins in the winter and put on my sunscreen in the summer. Getting older seems to mean more and more maintenance of the general body plant.

I'm glad that my spiritual body is a lot easier to maintain. In fact, it becomes stronger each day that I walk with the Lord. My faith deepens; my hope grows; my peace abides. The spiritual body thrives on daily use.

And the view just gets better and better on the upward journey!

Mentalpause
Laura Jensen Walker

I'm forty-two and having hot flashes.

What's up with *that*? I mean, forty-two??? C'mon! I thought that wasn't supposed to happen until I was around *sixty*-two.

My husband, Michael, who is three and a half years younger than I am, likes to joke, "I'm not even forty yet, and my wife is going through menopause."

But it's not just menopause, it's *mental*pause.

My memory is gone.

I'll be in the middle of an important conversation, start to begin a new sentence, and poof, it's vanished. Lost forever in the Bermuda triangle of mentalpause.

Or I can't remember names of common things around the house.

Like door.

Sink.

Husband.

I'll be explaining something to whatshisname, perhaps discussing a project that needs to get done, and the name of the item I'm discussing simply eludes me (although the project doesn't, much to my husband's dismay).

Finally, I point at the offending object in frustration and say, "Whatever that thing is called. You *know* what I'm talking about!"

Pointing has become my latest aerobic activity, and *whatchamacallit* is my noun of choice these days.

It's not as if my memory's ever been my greatest attribute. I've always had what my family would call "selective memory."

Or a vivid imagination.

My remembrances of the halcyon days of childhood in Wisconsin are never quite the same as the rest of my family's.

When my older sister Lisa and I were about seven and eight we took swimming classes at the "Y" downtown.

I can still recall the scent of chlorine and the sound of twelve pairs of bare little-girl feet slip-slapping on the wet hardwood floor alongside the pool as we made our way to the dreaded diving board.

We looked like a pack of penguins in our shiny one-piece black bathing suits and white rubber swim caps strapped snugly beneath our chins. Those tightly stretched skull caps gave off an overpowering rubber smell, which in concert with the chlorine was a potent combination, enough to make a young girl swoon—particularly if she hadn't had her afternoon snack yet.

Maybe that helps to explain what happened next.

Perhaps I was a little faint from all the "Y" aromas swirling about me so that when it came my turn to dive off the board, I

wasn't in perfect form. (Actually, I'm never in perfect form when diving—I prefer the one-handed jump method where my hand plugs my nose tightly shut to prevent water from whooshing up it.)

But that was many years later.

On this fateful day I was trying to be a good little girl and follow the diving directions.

Crack.

I hit my head on the bottom of the pool and had to be pulled to safety by the swimming instructor.

No wonder I'm not a water baby.

I stand, wearing only a towel and a blank look.
Michael, however, wears an entirely different look.

Years later, we were over at my folks' house one day when I first told my beloved about this traumatic childhood experience, and my mom burst out laughing.

Between snickers, she said, "Laura, that was ME. You never hit your head on the bottom of the pool when you were little—I did."

I'm really close to my mom so I guess I must have absorbed her childhood pain as my own.

See what they mean? Selective memory.

But at least that's better than no memory at all—which is what I have these days.

I'll get up from my desk to go to the kitchen for a glass of water, but halfway there, I forget what I got up for.

Can you relate?

Or I'll stride purposefully into the living room intending to pick up my latest *Victoria* magazine for a little soak-in-the-tub

reading, and this time I'll make it all the way into the room before the mentalpause hits.

So there I stand, wearing only a towel and a blank look.

Michael, however, wears an entirely different look.

Men and their one-track minds. At least he still has his mind.

But just wait 'til he turns forty.

True confession time: At the beginning of this story, I told you I was forty-two. Now I've never been one of those women who lie about their age. And I'm not now.

I just forgot that I'm forty-three.

Must have been a mentalpause moment.

Either that or this age thing is moving much faster than I realized.

But at least I'm in good company.

Even Michael suffers from mentalpause.

He says he needs one of those little hourglasses that comes up on the computer screen and says "processing" when someone asks him a question.

Or better yet, a blinking light like the Borg.

For those of you who aren't Star Trek fans, the Borg are bald, chalk-white robotic aliens—part-human, mostly machine—with all sorts of tubes and wires sticking out of their bodies and a light on their heads that blinks when they're assimilating information.

Wait a minute…that's the ticket. Everyone over forty just needs to get a blinking Borg light.

Then when they're having a mentalpause moment, at least people will know they're not lost in space on some distant planet.

How Did You Get So Old?

Helen Widger Middlebrooke

My firstborn, Matthew, is thirteen, and I am full of wonder.

I wonder how he got to be so old so fast. Thirteen already!? It seems just a breath ago I first whispered his name.

I wonder where the baby went. Where's the toothless smile, the innocent giggle, the hands that barely grasped a rattle? Now a young man strides through my house, looking very mature with a baby brother on his shoulder.

Where's the toddler who had a million questions, who sought me out when he needed wisdom? He's now a budding scientist with his own answers.

Somewhere between the booties and the Nikes, I must have fallen asleep. Or maybe I just wasn't watching closely enough. Sure, I saw changes—a lost tooth here, an outgrown shoe there— but in the busyness of life, I sometimes overlooked the bigger picture; he was a boy headed toward manhood.

Suddenly, he's thirteen and at the threshold. And I wonder: Is he prepared? Have I given him the tools he needs to forge his own life? Will he be equipped before he goes through the door in another five or six short years?

I wonder how he's become so much older, while I've hardly aged at all.

More than anything, I wonder how he's become so much older, while I've hardly aged at all. Why, aside from a few wrinkles, I look the same as I did the day he was born. (Okay, okay! Almost the same.)

Plus I've become wiser.

And so has he.

One morning he blindsided me.

"Mom! Your hair!"

I turned and looked at him, eye to eye. "What about it?"

"It's got gray in it!"

"It's been there awhile. You just didn't see it."

"But there's a lot of it! Especially on the side!"

"It comes with age. Like zits."

"Guys! Mom's got gray hair!"

I smiled and bit my tongue.

Yeah, he's thirteen all right.

Only five more years to go.

technology:
friend or foe?

You've Got Prayer!

A Sunday school teacher was teaching her class the Lord's Prayer. After a week of practice, she asked each child to stand and recite the Lord's Prayer individually. A little boy said, "Lead us not into temptation, but deliver us some E-mail."

—CAL AND ROSE SAMRA,
MORE HOLY HILARITY

Techno Babble

Charlene Ann Baumbich

I've had a few occasions arise that hurled me into a quest for cutting edge technology. Then again, one might refer to it as the crimped crease of archaic design, depending on your salesperson and their amenability to your desire to upgrade, yet cling to cognitive understanding.

Having a home office is a catalyst for much of my electronic angst. One of my most recent bouts of Technologically Induced Mental Mania (TIMM) was triggered by telephones. In fact, several rounds of telephone troubles have aimed their ammunition my way. My only consolation is that I'm not alone. Every time I engage in telling someone about my latest fiasco, they have five stories of their own. In fact, I bet you start talking to this book after reading a couple of mine.

You: You think that's something. Wait 'til I tell you about this.
Book: Silence.

You: (Scene 2. Stage right. Dark corner of mental institution—hours later.) You're slumped into a little wad, holding your ears because someone heard you talking to the book and had you carted away. Obsessed, you just kept talking, trying to cleanse yourself of all the irritations, Muzak tunes, disconnections, garbled fax messages, and answering machine marathons that still swim in your head. Meanwhile, similar diatribes begin spouting from the people who strapped on your straightjacket, forcing you to listen to them since you can't escape. And they all sound like prerecorded voice messages that don't respond to human utterings.

Technology. Just typing the word launched me into cyberspace, wherever that is.

A couple months ago I put an office line in. My home phone line just couldn't handle everything I needed it to do: modem, business calls, answering machine, fax, e-mail…

Actually, getting the second line wasn't too difficult; a handy friend helped us install it. However, it took several visits to phone stores, and multiple phone calls with other home office people, to try to figure out the actual mechanics of the situation. Which line should the answering machine be on? Did I care if business calls came in on my home line? (I didn't really want to have to change all my letterhead and business cards.) Should the fax machine be on standby? How would I recognize its ring? Or did I even want to know if and when it was ringing?

As it turned out, I was forced to leave the fax ringer off because the number for my new business line had been freshly abandoned by someone who let their dog run loose and he was still running, and people were still mad. Each time I'd turn the ringer on, the phone immediately started ringing with angry

people calling about all kinds of mad things. You'd think they'd be tired of the fax signal by now.

After much consternation, deliberation, and hair pulling, I decided to get a two-line phone for my office. The answering machine would stay on the home phone in the kitchen because that's where George is used to looking for it. Besides, that combination phone and answering machine and recorder was relatively new, and I hadn't recovered from that last TIMM bout yet. All the digital versus tape, two tapes versus one, separate answering machine versus built-in, and stuff like that could very easily trigger another attack.

Okay, stay with me here: The kitchen phone/answering machine/recorder stayed in the kitchen; the two-line phone went in my office and the phone on the fax stayed dormant.

Then I realized it would also be wise to have the business line in the kitchen because I often get myself a drink or snack or stare out the window into my backyard when I'm on business calls. Nothing personal, just a habit. So the old office phone got hung on the wall

*Technology.
Just typing the
word launched me
into cyberspace,
wherever that is.*

in the kitchen right above the old (but relatively new) combo home phone-answering machine that sat on a stand. Thus, the set-up for disaster.

One unsuspecting day, I initiated a call from my kitchen on my business line and was chatting away when, Riiiiing. Riiiing. "Hold on. It's my other line," I said to Call Number One. I pushed the hold button and set the cradle on my left shoulder.

"Hello" I said to Caller Number Two on my home phone.

The person identified herself, but before I could say, "I'll call you back," my call waiting signal rang in.

"Hold on, please," I said to Caller Number Two. I pushed the flash button and said "Hello" to Caller Number Three.

My head was swimming. I couldn't think. I was breaking a sweat, and all I could think to say to Caller Number Three was, "Hold on a moment, please." I set that phone cradle on my right shoulder and tried to pull myself together. I felt like I was living the Who's On First comedy routine.

I ended up taking everyone's number and said I'd call them back, even the first person whom I'd called. It occurred to me that, while I was engaged in decorating myself with cradles and cords, I still didn't have enough lines to operate my fax or my modem at that particular moment. Amazing.

But I truly became amazed when I opened my mailbox and received three phone bills on the same day: home line, business line, and car phone. "The phone company owns me," I said to George. He groaned. The sum total of those bills is as incomprehensible as trying to figure out how it happens that my toilet seat seems to be mysteriously wired to my phone line. The minute my backside hits the circle, the phone rings.

You know, there's something to be said for an outhouse in the country. Away from the hustle and bustle. And the telephone.

Caller I.Q.

Marilyn Meberg

A year ago I finally yielded to the social pressure to buy a cell phone. I find cell phones exceedingly annoying, but one would of course be helpful in the event I'm ever stuck in Bisbee, Arizona; Fargo, North Dakota; or Maud, Texas. I suppose I would want to let someone know my location. Actually, I'm not sure who would be interested in knowing my whereabouts, but it is comforting to contemplate the possibility.

The fact that I'm technologically challenged was the major hindrance to purchasing a phone. However, my friend and technical consultant, Pat Wenger, explained how it worked, and I reluctantly became a cell-phone owner.

Things were going moderately well until the word "edit" appeared inexplicably at the bottom of the screen several days after the purchase. No matter which button I selected, "edit" would not disappear. Now frankly, I've never felt inclined toward

that word. It conjures up images of a book editor's red-marking my manuscripts with the familiar criticism "too wordy." But the possibility that even my phone conversations might be subject to editing seemed utterly unreasonable.

Having punched every available button, I gave up editing "edit" and attempted to call my friend Luci. A male voice answered. That didn't fit. I said, "I'm sorry, I guess I punched in the wrong number." He pleasantly replied, "Don't be sorry"…long pause…then, "Mare Bear??" I responded, "Unco Neal??" It was my brother-in-law in Colorado!

I told him that I had a new phone that I had not yet mastered and that how I got him (he's an *A* for Atkinson and Luci's an *S* for Swindoll) was a mystery. Neil is well aware of my mechanical deficit and knew better than to try to figure it out with me. We had a wonderful visit and hung up. I didn't try to call Luci again…I figured Neil was too busy.

The next day, comforted by the mysterious disappearance of the word "edit," I decided to call Pat. Scrolling through the alphabet with the right-hand button, I punched in "Wenger" and waited. Nothing…no sound…nada. Holding the maddening little phone in the palm of my hand I walked over to my desk to see if the instruction booklet made any more sense than it had the day before. It didn't.

Muttering peevishly about the possibility of banishing my phone to live in solitary confinement with my two computers, I faintly heard my name. I was alone in the room. With deliberate enunciation I kept hearing, "Marilyn…Mar…i…lyn." I looked uncomprehendingly at my phone. The voice was coming from it. Putting the phone to my ear I tentatively said, "What?" It was Neil. He was laughing so hard he could barely talk. He was hear-

ing my muffled mutterings and of course knew what had happened yet again. We had another pleasant conversation punctuated every now and then with guffaws of laughter (his, not mine).

Later in the day I decided to call Marge (Neil's wife and Ken's sister) to giggle together over my latest flash of technological genius. Thinking it'd be a cinch to call her since I'd connected with their number so effortlessly before, I punched "Atkinson." Pat Wenger answered.

My technical missteps add spice to my life and keep me on my toes. However, it is also true that I'm a bit embarrassed by myself. Small children click and mouse along effortlessly with their computers; the world chatters endlessly on cell phones, not one of which manages to connect with my brother-in-law in Colorado.

The possibility that even my phone conversations might be subject to editing seemed utterly unreasonable.

What's Marilyn's problem? Who exactly knows how to explain the faulty wiring in my brain that short-circuits my efforts to master technology? That frankly is not my concern! But in all seriousness, what is a concern is how I feel. Embarrassment has its roots in shame. But if we love ourselves unconditionally, then even when we blow it badly, making huge or small mistakes, we do not waver in our agreement with God that we are still lovable—because He says we are!

More Things, More Holders

Marti Attoun

It's no wonder I'm unorganized. I simply don't have enough "thing" holders.

And, no, Mom, I don't want detergent boxes and plastic milk jugs sawed in half or empty bean cans to hold my pencils and possessions.

I'm talking high-dollar thing holders: wire shelf systems with scaffolding creeping along every inch of closet and cubes and pigeonholes on wheels and baskets and pockets in wood, cloth and plastic. There's no end to the clever shapes and sizes and they're in stores everywhere. In fact, complete stores are devoted to handsome thing holders.

And, if you can afford it, you can hire a professional who will assess your thing-holding needs and customize your thing holders.

I know that getting rid of "mess stress" is the key to happiness because all my women's magazines say so every month.

So I bought a three-story plastic rolling bin for the kitchen. I figured I'd start by filing my onions and potatoes, get a taste of success and work my way up to the laundry and office mess.

Before the day was over, some wise guy had polluted my system by sticking three pieces of mail into the purple onion bin.

"Excuse me," I said, waving the electric bill. "This particular thing holder is for vegetables only. The bills go in the wooden pigeonholes in my office, two across and three down."

From the way the wise guy looked at me, I could tell he was impressed.

"We're wasting too much precious time hunting for things. Little by little, every thing in this house will have its own holder."

Once this container craze gets you in its grip, there's no putting a lid on it. For example, my things-to-do basket now sits beside the telephone near the yellow plastic crate that holds the telephone books and address book. I'm thinking of transferring the yellow crate to the bathroom, though, for towels

Once this container craze gets you in its grip, there's no putting a lid on it.

and topping it with a handy turntable for shampoos and such. I could use one of the wire stacking baskets for the phone book.

When my husband hunted for his car keys this morning, I proudly directed him to a series of cloth wall pockets hanging inside the hall closet door. These are similar to the cheap vinyl shoe pockets Mom used years ago.

Actually, cloth pockets of various sizes stitched to every piece of furniture and hanging on every wall is the ideal way to go. These pocket systems are already available for the backs of car seats and the sides of recliners.

I'm thinking big now, but I may contact my sewing buddy Juanita to see if she can stitch up some giant house pockets to hang on every wall and hallway. There'd be no excuse then for being unorganized.

Well, one. We'd still need to remember which thing holder held which thing. And I'm sure I'd end up with a potato in my sock thing holder.

Perhaps I'll just throw away all my things and keep the thing holders.

There, I feel more organized already.

a pound of laughter

What If You Bicycled in Reverse to Ben & Jerry's?

If you jogged backwards, would you gain weight?

—RICHARD W. BIMLER AND
ROBERT D. BIMLER,
LET THERE BE LAUGHTER

Weighty Matters
Patsy Clairmont

Scales that announce your weight? You've got to be kidding! How humiliating. I bet some ninety-pound, undernourished model came up with that winner.

The only thing worse than a robot announcing my tonnage is a robot with recall.

I was staying with my friends, the Hootens in El Paso, when Joyce announced, "Patsy, we have a new scale you must try."

"Oh, really," I replied with skepticism. "Why is that?"

"It's just wonderful. It talks," she joyfully reported. "It will not only tell you your weight, but it also has a memory and will tell you tomorrow if you have lost or gained."

She was thrilled. I was appalled.

I find it depressing to think that, as Righteous Robot trumpets my weight, everyone in the home hears the results. This isn't the final score for the World Series, for goodness' sakes.

"Patsy has gained five and a half pounds!" I imagined it broadcasting.

Yes, it even calls you by name.

I believe in being friendly, but calling me by my first name in the same breath as my weight is a little too intimate for me.

Next they'll put a microchip in our driver's license that heralds our age every time we pull it out of our wallets.

Calling me by my first name in the same breath as my weight is a little too intimate for me.

After a number of creative stalls, I finally responded, "No, Joyce, I'm only here for a few days. I don't think it would be productive."

Translated that means, "Ain't no way I'm leaving Texas with that information left behind."

Crash Diet at Freeway Speeds

Karen Scalf Linamen

I've been off my diet for weeks.

This morning my breakfast consisted of cookies and potato chips. The good news is the chips were of the low-fat variety. The bad news is that I ate half a bag.

Wait. It gets worse.

Then, a couple hours ago I found myself in the drive-through lane at McDonald's. But it TOTALLY wasn't my fault. After forgetting to pack a lunch for my teenager, I promised to deliver a sandwich to her school office. When I realized I didn't have any bread in the house, I found myself forced to drive through McDonald's and purchase a cheeseburger and fries for her. And, as you can well imagine, the only way to keep myself from eating her French fries while I drove was to buy a second burger and fries of my very own.

The next thing I know I'm driving down the highway and smelling French fries and salivating at the thought of chasing down my breakfast of cookies and chips with a nice, greasy burger when suddenly I think to myself:

LINAMEN, GET A GRIP!

Sure, I started a diet on January 1 just like you did. But here I am, already two weeks strong into a hearty binge.

Say it ain't so.

You know, starting a diet is one thing. Starting it for the eighty-seventh time gets a little tedious.

Anyway, I was thinking about all this while driving down the freeway when suddenly I got the strong urge to take charge of my life and climb back on the rabbit food wagon, forsaking greasy pleasures for celery and salads. I almost chucked my cheeseburger out the window until I realized that the only thing worse than starting a diet for the eighty-seventh time would be starting a diet for the eighty-seventh time AND having to pay a $200 littering fine to boot.

> The only thing worse than starting a diet for the eighty-seventh time would be starting a diet for the eighty-seventh time AND having to pay a $200 littering fine to boot.

A few minutes later I walked into Kaitlyn's school office carrying two sacks. I dropped one sack on Mrs. Crumpton's desk and waved the other. "Does anyone want a burger and fries?"

Mrs. Stracener said, "Did they give you an extra one?"

"Nope. It's mine." And then I blurted the whole ugly story, about the chips and the cookies and the two-week binge and realizing I needed to GET A GRIP and feeling desperate and nearly getting fined for littering—

About that time Mrs. Crumpton grabbed my hands, looked solidly into my eyes, and said reassuringly, "We can help you, dear."

"Thank you!" I gushed. "Just don't let me eat the fries…whatever you do, DON'T LET ME EAT THE FRIES!"

So now I'm back on my diet, and there are two women in Texas who think what I really should be on is medication.

I hate starting over. It doesn't matter if the thing I'm starting over is a diet or a page of prose that I should have had saved when my dog tripped over the electrical cord to my computer. The other thing I hate to do is start over when I stumble in my walk with Jesus. Somehow, I'd love to deal with a sin or doubt or fear or struggle once and never have to deal with it again. I'd love to announce—when the topic of gossip or lust or envy comes up— "Been there, done that!"

I'd love to say, "Anger? Oh Sure. I got angry back in 1974, but the Lord delivered me, and I've been gracious ever since."

"Depression? Did that in '87. Never struggled since."

"Lack of faith? Lord and I put that one to bed back in '93."

The good news is that even when I'm feeling defeated from having to muster a brand-new attack on a not-so-new enemy, there's Someone standing by with fresh resources to see me through. Indeed, the Bible promises us that God's mercies and compassion never fail. In fact, they are new every morning, and his faithfulness is great!

Even when I'm weak, he is strong.

Which is reassuring. Especially since I only ate half the bag of chips this morning. I think the other half is still waiting for me in the kitchen.

George and Charlene in the Garden of Calories

Charlene Ann Baumbich

This is the first time in our marriage that my husband and I have been Chunkos together. Chunkos translated: pudgies, fluffies, middle-aged spreadies.

Although we have each taken numerous turns acquiring the rather unlofty title of Chunko, we have never been so unfortunate as to have found ourselves there together. Our huge box of photographs is a visible reminder of this truth, but, unfortunately, those pictures are in the same state we are: overflowing.

The first episode of the four-letter word that starts with "D" and ends with "T" came before we were married. George was eating nothing but boiled eggs, drinking water by the barge-load, and driving throughout the country looking for a little-known commodity called farmer's cheese.

I, on the other hand, had been successful at weight reduction several years previous by existing solely on carrot sticks and steak.

Of course, by today's cholesterol standards, we should both be dead, not thin—and we are neither, at least as of this writing.

As our nuptials approached, I lost more weight and glued on fake fingernails in an attempt to look dreamy in the wedding pictures. Something I probably would have accomplished had it not been for my dorky taste in headpieces and the fact that all but two of my glue-on nails were off for the hand-on-hand photo.

During this same period, George was the first to, ahem, blossom. Truthfully, I think perhaps he'd already started before the vows; probably a slingshot reaction to finally finding the farmer's cheese. Nevertheless, on our wedding day, George was up and I was down when it came to body elasticity.

When we are at our natural weights, which we can no longer remember, we are opposites anyway: George is six-foot, two inches with a large (size thirteen shoe) frame, and I am five-foot, three-and-a-half inches with a medium frame. Okay. Maybe a medium-large frame, but you get the picture.

Somewhere along the line, we started exchanging Chunkodom status: George shrank and I expanded. This became brutally clear on a fishing trip. I had to wear a pair of his jeans for half a day and they fit! Oh sure, childbearing had perhaps expanded my hips, but relentless bags of crunchy snacks had turned my thighs tank-size.

Now that I think about it, perhaps that was how we stayed opposites. One got thin because the other was actually consuming every bag and package of junk food in sight; thereby shutting the door to temptation for the other.

Eventually a high blood-sugar scare sobered me into an exchange-list diet. Fear incites self-discipline, I learned. Once again, I shrank…but George mysteriously expanded.

In reality it wasn't a mystery at all. George was always called upon to finish what was left on my plate that didn't fit my diet. I'm telling you, I had amazing control. I didn't even lick frosting off my fingers when baking birthday cakes.

And then my blood sugar leveled. And that was the end of denying myself edible goodies. About the time George decided he was going to join me in svelteness, I was no longer motivated by the threat of death.

And so the story goes, and goes, and goes, until…here we are, Chunkos together.

One would think that dieting together would make life easier. After all: Misery loves company. If I'm going to be miserable because I blew it and polished off the Cheetos, why shouldn't he be filled with the same guilt? There's always another bag to wave in front of him. And if he has been a bad boy in terms of caloric intake, why shouldn't he buy me Charleston Chew candy bars for a surprise? (Something that told me he loved me even though I was a Chunko—this really delighted me until he suggested that we *share* the chocolate.)

These days, if he tried to finish the leftover food on my plate—which, of course, there never is—I would undoubtedly pierce his hand with my fork. If I suggest he not mound that second helping on his plate, he would undoubtedly stand up— stretching his king-size frame to the max—and dare me to stop him.

The more we think and talk about "having to do something about this," the more we are focused on food. Buttered popcorn. "Want some, hon? I'll make it." Pizza. "What a day! Let's just call out." Candy. "Better finish this off so it's not here to tempt us."

We have no one to set an inspiring example. We have no reason to feel, "Gee, I shouldn't let myself go since my spouse is in such wonderful shape." We have no shame.

What we have, however, is plenty of chiding. Even though we lure each other into our sinful feasting, we take pleasure in noticing and pointing out the other's shortcomings. Always a good way to ignore self.

"Don't tell me about my double chin," I chastise, "when I have an entire stack of your britches to sew because the crotch ripped out!"

"You're the one who grocery shops and buys this junk," he snaps back.

"So I didn't buy the junk this week and look at you! You're pilfering the dark side of the pantry!"

What we don't say and do blatantly, we find great pleasure and challenge in hiding and seeking. I have become a regular Sherlock Holmes at detecting George's telltale breadcrumbs and the peanut butter smears he deposits in the wee hours of the night. And he has discovered my hidden stashes—and takes edible advantage of them, I might add.

In the meantime, we roll our Chunko bodies in front of the television, pig out, and talk about getting serious about "this" tomorrow. All the while, "this" gets bigger.

And so we have to do something about "this."

No. We each have to be accountable for ourselves. After all, we've done it time and again. George and I agree. We should. We must. We owe it to ourselves and each other.

All we have to do is polish off this bag of pretzels, and then we'll be ready. Right, Dear?

11

mama mia
—more humor for moms

Jesus Perks Me Right Up

A three-year-old put her ear to her mother's chest.

"I'm listening to Jesus in your heart."

The woman permitted the little girl to listen for a few seconds, and then she asked, "Well, what did you hear?"

The child replied, "Sounds like He's making coffee to me."

—DR. JAMES DOBSON,
STORIES OF THE HEART AND HOME

Germs of Endearment

Becky Freeman

Who in their right mind would willingly hold out their hand to accept donations of a half-chewed Tootsie Roll, a freshly blown tissue, or a wriggling worm?

Who rushes to comfort a child with a virus, knowing full well that as soon as she reaches that child, her robe will be wearing the remains of last night's predigested pizza?

Who finally succumbs to the unrelenting choruses of "Isn't he cute?" and "We'll promise to feed him," only to awake some sub-zero morning to the reality that the fur-that-followed-them-home is now her sole responsibility?

Who else but, of course, our mothers.

Robert Fulghum described the one person in his house that sent him into orbits of awe because "she could reach into the sink with her bare hands—BARE HANDS" and pick up the lethal gunk from the sink drain. To top that, he once saw her

"reach into the wet garbage bag and fish around in there looking for a lost teaspoon BAREHANDED—a kind of mad courage. She found the spoon in a cup of coffee grounds mixed with scrambled egg remains and the end of the vegetable soup." Fulghum adds, "I almost passed out when she handed it to me to rinse off."

Without a doubt, we all know, this brave woman had to be none other than young Robert's mom.

Whose saliva can slick back the wildest curl, clean the toughest jelly stains from a five-year-old's cheek, and promptly cure infectious lesions?

Who can talk on the phone, fold a diaper with one hand, scold a child with one raised eyebrow, and elbow the front door closed while performing two sets of leg lifts?

Who runs in a panic when her toddler squeals to "See what I've done!" and breathes an enormous sigh of relief when she discovers the excitement is over a properly pooped-in potty?

Who calms all fears, cleans dirty ears, and though she grows weary, also grows more dear through the years?

Who exchanged the Days of Wine and Roses for Nights of Whines and Runny Noses?

No one else, of course, but our mothers.

With this impressive resumé behind our own mothers, what choice did we have when we reached grownuphood but to follow in her maternal house shoes, bear children, and become mothers as well? However, we found that parenthood was far from an instant success. It required education, experience, and multitudes of long-distance phone calls to Mother.

I recall three times in my life when I profoundly needed a mommy: when I was six and woke up with a bad dream; when

the girls in fourth grade wouldn't play with me; and when I was 20 years old and left all alone with my firstborn child for the first time. Maternity loomed like eternity. I took one look at that fragile child sleeping blissfully in his crib, unaware of the danger he was in, and realized with profound finality that he was wholly dependent on me for his continued existence. I felt I at least owed him some explanation of the bind we were in and how I planned to get us through it.

"Look kiddo," I whispered to Zach's sleeping form, "I know I look awfully young and naive to be taking on this Mommy Job. But hang in there. Don't move. Don't wake up. Don't ANYBODY PANIC! I can call in a professional Real Mommy if things start to get out of hand and I forget where I leave you, or feed you a jar of cold cream instead of baby food, or put toothpaste on your diaper rash."

I felt I at least owed him some explanation of the bind we were in and how I planned to get us through it.

Thankfully, my mother adapted to her role as Granny with near euphoria and proceeded to show me how to feed and bathe my little charge and, perhaps most importantly, how to communicate in newbornese. This involved holding the gazing baby with his head resting in the palm of my right hand and, using a high-pitched voice, speaking in a language that sounded one-third English, one-third Pig Latin, and one-third Cajun. "How's our witzy, bitzy, baby boy doin' dis mornin', huh? Dat's right, dat's right— you done blowed a good wittle bubble-y with your moufy, didn't you?"

With my mother's expert coaching, I became a passably good mother myself in a relatively short amount of time. I didn't misplace

my baby, I never mistook cold cream for baby food, and only once did I accidentally mix up the toothpaste with diaper ointment. Scott still remembers the shock of a mouth full of Desitin. ("But admit it," I told him years later, "you never had one oral outbreak of diaper rash, now did you?")

As my first baby grew and others arrived to keep him company, I found myself mixing and mingling with other mothers like the pro I'd become. Why, I could pack a diaper bag in less than five seconds, make a peanut butter sandwich so good it would halt a child in mid-whine. I could anticipate a toddler's runny "ker-choo!" with a ready tissue, and leap a pile of Legos with a single bound. (If you've never stepped on a Lego in the dark of night, well, let's just say one does learn how to leap.)

I could make a peanut butter sandwich so good it would halt a child in mid-whine.

When I survived the month-long Invasion of the Chicken Pox, and at least 24 midnight "Mom-meee, I'm sick at my tummmmeeeeeeeee!" calls, I knew I had earned my mommy merit badge and could hold my own in any Play Group.

Now I'm 40 years old. How did that *happen?* In two short months, my first-born son will be 20. (*That's* how it happened. My child aged me.) Zachary will be the same age that I was when I became his mother. Wow. It's so hard to believe. My baby, given the right circumstances—like a wife and a job—could have a baby of his own.

Currently, thankfully, Zach is single and still finding his way in this world. Marriage and babies seem a long way off in some far distant future, to him.

But today he dropped by for a brief visit and told me how he'd begun to enjoy a couple of his friends' little babies. How he loved holding them and jiggling them up and down until they giggled and burped. How soft their skin was and how trusting they were of the big people around them.

"Someday..." he said with a far-off look in his eyes.

"Someday..." I answered. "And, Zach, you'll be a wonderful father."

"Thanks, Mom," he replied, with a grateful grin.

I stood up, patted his shoulder, feeling peacefully serene in my role as "Mom/Someday Granny."

Then I rolled up my sleeves, walked toward the kitchen, and as a silent gesture of gratitude to my own mother (alias "Someday Great-Granny") resolutely fished the goop out of the drain, BAREHANDED.

The Great Diaper Derby

Chonda Pierce

At one point in time, David and I believed that if we had a two-week supply of diapers, everything would be just great. So imagine our surprise when we discovered, while strolling through the mall one evening, a baby race that provided the winner with a two-weeks' supply of disposable diapers—and not those cheap, store-brand kind that gave Chera diaper rash.

David held Chera in his arms while I filled out an entry form. "Are you sure she's up to this?" I asked. After all, she was only fifteen months old. But David reminded me that she had started to walk at nine months, so she had a good six months' experience.

When we finished the paperwork, we were given a big, sticky number four that we stuck to the back of her tiny shirt. We were directed to the far end of a cushy mat that was about fifteen feet long and divided into six lanes by white stripes.

I heard David talking to Chera about "visualizing victory"

and "running like a gazelle." But all I could think of was what if my little baby ran over the white line, bumped noggins with another runner, and knocked loose the only tooth she had—the one we were so proud of. If she lost the race, would she be traumatized forever? Was the mat soft enough? Had they used a disinfectant to clean it after the last race? Did anyone think about cleaning it at all?

A young woman (who was surely way too young to have children of her own) wearing a ponytail and chewing gum explained the race's rules. "First of all, I'd like to welcome all of you to the Great Diaper Derby here at Hickory Hollow Mall. Since I don't speak baby language—hee hee—let me explain to the contestants' parents how this race is supposed to go. To start out, one parent will stand at this end of the mat with your child in your respective lane." She pointed to the end of the mat where we already were standing. Each lane was marked with a number between one and six.

"The other parent is welcome to stand or sit at the finish line and call your child to you. You can call, clap, sing, whatever it takes, but do not touch or reach across the line to drag your child across."

It was time to take our positions, so David finished massaging Chera's legs (while she giggled) and took his place at the finish line. He got on his hands and knees and made faces at her, causing her to giggle more. She tried to squirm from my arms to run to him, and David called back, "Oh, that's good. That's real good, Chera. Channel that! Channel that!"

We had stripped Chera down to just a diaper and a shirt—no shoes or socks on the mat, David had said. "That'll only slow her down. She needs to feel the wind between her toes."

I tightly held on to Chera and waited for the girl with the gum and ponytail to start the race. That gave me a chance to size up the competition. After a quick look around, I began to think my baby just might win this thing. "Run like a gazelle!" I wanted to shout, but decided not to.

We were in lane four. Next to us, on the far left in lanes one and two, were twin boys with big, curly hair. They were both sitting—despite what their hairless father kept shouting at them from the finish line. One was even chewing on the end of his shoe and therefore wasn't positioned for a quick start. Racer number three was crying and trying to get her mom to pick her up. Her mom kept pushing her back down and telling her to run like she did at home whenever Grandpa would take his teeth out and try to bite her with them. But the thoughts of that just made the toddler cry even more.

In lane five was a contestant who couldn't even walk yet—or if she could, she preferred to crawl. (Earlier I had noticed that whenever she crawled to a wall or table, her mom would pick her up and point her in the right direction, as if she were a box turtle.) Finally, in lane six was a child with a very runny nose, very runny.

The girl with the ponytail and chewing gum shouted, "On your marks!"

I wanted to call time-out and wipe racer number six's nose myself.

"Get set!"

I whispered in Chera's ear, "Run to Daddy when I say so, Chera." She was already squirming and trying to pull free.

"Go!"

I let go, and Chera bolted down the mat like a...*like a gazelle!* David was red faced and calling her to him, fanning the air, pulling Chera along in the draft. Her little, naked feet pitter-pattered across the germ-laden rubber mat, sounding like rain-drops. She was only two steps away from the finish line when I realized how badly I wanted those diapers, when I realized that this was how God was going to provide for us. "Go, Chera! Go! Run like the—"

She stopped.

And the wind stuck in my throat, as all I could do was watch. David's arm kept pinwheeling, creating a breeze that blew back his hair, but Chera would not budge. Instead, she stood there and stared at her father (probably at the little blue vein that pops up on his forehead whenever he gets excited).

"Come on to Daddy," David grunted, his arm spinning at the shoulder joint like a puppet's. "Come across this line for your surprise! Come on. I'll give you a piece of candy. How about some ice cream? Wouldn't you like some ice cream? Come on across the line. No more naps—ever! Just cross the line!"

David was starting to embarrass me. In the meantime, the twins were off and running; however, they opted to run diago-nally. The one that had been chewing his shoe earlier led the way for a bit. But his shoelace had come untied and he stepped on it, tripping into lane three and sliding all the way to lane five. His brother was right behind him, and together they wound up in lane six—crying. Their hairless father was jangling his car keys in hopes that would attract them, but the one who had found his shoe earlier found it again and began to chew.

The crying girl in lane three who wanted her mommy never

did get going. In fact, she just cried louder and louder. Her dad had even pulled an Oreo cookie from his pocket and was waggling it in the air. This only made her cry more.

The runny-nosed kid nearly got us both disqualified when he made a beeline for Chera. With his arms pulled back, shoulders raised, and (runny) nose first, he took at least a dozen baby steps toward Chera and was about to crash into her (doctor's bills, antibiotics—I could see it all coming) when he suddenly veered off toward the Oreo cookie that was meant for the crying racer who only wanted her mommy. He blindsided the father and snatched away the cookie.

Well, this only made the crying kid in lane three more furious, and she wailed so loud that I couldn't hear David on the other end but I could read his lips. "Come on, Chera. I'll give you a car! A house! Half of my kingdom!"

But Chera wouldn't budge. She just stood there, two steps from crossing the line, and stared at David, who I was afraid would pass out—if not that, he was in the process of giving away everything we ever owned (and a lot we didn't) for the sake of two weeks' worth of diapers.

In the midst of the screaming, the fanning, the cookies, the snot, and the teething, one little baby moved steadily forward on all fours, past the crying baby in lane three, past the twins (who were both chewing on their own—and each other's—shoes and had sprawled out in lanes four, five, and six), past the runny-nosed kid, who now had a combination of snot and Oreos all over his face, and even past Chera, who could have been a statue placed there to face her father. The little child who crawled everywhere crawled right up into her father's arms and began to pull at his nose. I watched the father hold his baby and close his eyes—

probably dreaming of the two-weeks' supply of diapers stacked in a corner of the baby's room.

With the race over, David reached out and gathered Chera in his arms and began to talk to her. The big vein in his forehead had returned to normal, and his face wasn't as red. I walked up and heard him saying to her, "Shake it off. You'll get 'em next time. Hey, you can't win 'em all."

I put Chera's socks and shoes back on her feet as quickly as I could and noticed that no one was disinfecting the mat to prepare for the next race.

On the way home David stopped at 7-11 and bought us all ice cream cones and Chera a pack of diapers, enough to last her about four days. To pay for the diapers, he would have to work about two hours and probably would have to get pretty greasy. (He was a heating and air conditioning mechanic.)

It seemed like such an easy way to meet our needs, I thought. *Win the race and get free diapers.* I tried to make myself think that maybe the crawling baby from lane number five needed them more than we did.

For a couple of days, I wondered why God hadn't met our needs when we had given him such an easy opportunity to do so. But only for a couple of days, because after that it turned cold and pipes all over town froze and burst. David worked lots of overtime, enough to buy lots and lots of diapers—and we did.

God always has met our needs, but rarely in the ways I think he will or even should. But after all, he is God, and he has great plans for his children—crying ones, whiny ones, fast ones, slow ones, and ones with runny noses—and his plans don't always include winning a Great Diaper Derby in the mall.

White Can Wait

Gwendolyn Mitchell Diaz

I'll never quite understand why, but God ordained me to be the mother of four extremely noisy, perpetually active sons. In addition, He blessed me with a male dog; two stray cats (both male); a pair of hamsters which have never produced any offspring (so I can only guess)…and then, of course, there's my husband—the one who started it all!

With all these "Y" chromosomes wandering around the house, I find myself missing out on many of the daintier, frillier things in life. I find it hard to justify owning fine china, fancy curtains, and lace doilies while there are five mud-cleated, soda-splattering, sweaty-smelling males (plus their friends *and* animals) lounging from one end of my house to the other.

I have been dragged to every sporting event and war movie in history. I've watched countless males get gory and "grody." I have yet to find myself seated at a ballet with any of my four sons

besides me watching pink swirls of grace and grandeur. (I gave up trying to get my husband to accompany me years ago when I realized that his idea of a cultural event was a professional wrestling match at the Civic Center.)

I miss ceramic rabbits with bows sitting on my windowsills; padded, lace-covered picture albums decorating my coffee table; or flowery placemats accenting, say, a fluffy quiche. And it is with great wistfulness that I recall having once had a wonderful relationship with the color white...

White—as in magnolia blossoms picked early in the morning and set in a china bowl on the breakfast table.

White—as in crisp, cool cotton sheets and spotless lace tablecloths.

White—as in clean, freshly painted, unmarked family room walls.

White—as in the wedding gown, so pure and simple, that got me into all this!

One day, as I was hunting through the summer sales racks, I spied a pair of white shorts. They were sharp. Cool. Clean. Crisp. And just the right size. I *had* to have them!

With all these "Y" chromosomes wandering around the house, I find myself missing out on many of the daintier, frillier things in life.

That evening I bravely donned my new, white shorts and set out for the baseball field. The world took on a new feeling, and I took on a completely new air as I strutted into the ballpark. I felt chic. Proper. Special!

I realized I would have to make some adjustments to keep my fresh, white act together. And I was ready. I firmly kept Ben at arm's length while he ate his purple slushy. Jonathan was not

allowed to sit anywhere close to me after diving under the bleachers for a foul ball. Zach and Matthew had to hold their own baseball gear, for once, while they balanced their sodas and pizza after the game. And I refrained from ketchup on my hot dog—just in case.

White is worth it, I thought smugly to myself as I got up to leave…only to find myself—and my new white shorts—attached to the metal bleachers by a huge glob of gooey pink bubble gum!

I have now resigned myself to the fact that white and motherhood are incompatible. I guess white will have to wait!

12

adolescent amusement

Hidden Motivation

My neighbor Everett finally hit upon a way to get his sixteen-year-old son to mow the lawn: "I told him I lost the car keys in the tall grass."

—LOWELL D. STREIKER,
A TREASURY OF HUMOR

Know When to Say No, Part 1

Helen Widger Middlebrooke

I should have said no.

There wasn't time for a haircut—he had to catch the camp bus in thirty minutes. Besides, for two years he had said buzz cuts look stupid.

But I said yes. So he sat down on the kitchen stool amid the rising tide of siblings.

I went to work with the clippers: Up the back, up the sides. Step over the baby.

I stopped. "You're sure you want it all buzzed?"

"I'm sure."

Back to work: Off the top with the thick, red hair. Step around the baby. Move the preschooler. One more stroke and—

OOPS!

The guide came off the clippers! In a split second I had made a hole in his haircut! He had been fuzzed, not buzzed!

"Get me a wig! I can't go to camp like this!"

Wailing, I left the room to let his father deal with the problem.

When the tears subsided, we sent him to camp under a ball cap, which would stay on all week. But after one hot afternoon, he decided to get fuzzed all over. I got him a cooler Aussie-style bush hat. He felt a little better.

But I still felt guilty. I had ruined my ten year old's life for camp week. I made a mistake, but he paid for it. Would he ever forgive me? Would he be forever maladjusted for having spent the summer looking like a grunt? What had I done?

Mother-guilt is very inhibiting. And there's so much of it around today. Thanks to the experts, we modern moms think our every action will mar our kids for life.

Yes, we can make serious, life-changing errors. But most mistakes are not forever. Kids are more resilient than we think.

I know, because my mom once made a mistake. She accidentally gave me aspirin and almost killed me. But I survived the allergic reaction, and I forgave her.

Some day after summer's end, my son will forgive me.

Then he'll find a new barber.

I am not perfect, Father,
sometimes I fail, sometimes I offend.
Sometimes those offenses hurt my children.
Help me to be humble before my little ones
that I may restore their confidence in me.
And let us all find grace to help in time of need.

Cats Can't Baby-sit

Gwendolyn Mitchell Diaz

It was a Tuesday evening. The baseball team had just won a huge game. Everyone on the team was jumping around, giving each other high five's—everyone except my fifteen-year-old, that is. He approached me with a downcast, forlorn look on his face.

"What's the matter?" I needed to know. "Why aren't you excited? Your team just won!"

"Yeah, but I also just failed my fifth period exploratory wheel class," he mumbled dejectedly. "I left my stupid 'egg kids' home without a baby-sitter!"

I didn't have a clue what he was talking about. I wondered if the hit he had taken when he slid into base during the second inning had scrambled his brains.

"What on earth is an egg kid?" I demanded.

He filled me in. Apparently, at school that day each student had been given an egg. For three days they were to be responsible

for it as though it were a real child. They were to treat it gently and take it with them wherever they went. The eggs had come with little felt caps and silly felt-tip smiles. Much to his chagrin, the only set of twins had been placed in my son's custodial care.

He had brought his egg babies home that afternoon in a little basket filled with Easter grass and immediately shoved them in the fridge. The last place he ever expected to run into his teacher was at the ball field that night. But there she was, and sometime around the sixth inning, she managed to ask him through the dugout fence where his egg twins were. She let him know in no uncertain terms that, "Home, chillin' in the fridge," was not an acceptable answer.

"Egg kids are a real pain. You've got to drag them with you wherever you go!"

"You weren't really serious, were you?" he asked. "You didn't really expect me to bring eggs with faces on them to the ball field? Besides, they're a whole lot safer in the fridge than they would be out here. Do you know what a foul ball can do to an egg?" He quickly reasoned.

His teacher wasn't the least bit amused by his logic. "It's considered child abuse to leave your babies unattended," she responded quite seriously. "I'll have to mark your grade way down!"

"Child abuse! That's ridiculous!" He was more than a little perturbed. "Anyway, I didn't leave them home unattended. The cat is taking care of them."

She shook her head, "I'm afraid cats can't function as baby-sitters," she responded quite curtly.

"Hey, if eggs can be babies, why can't cats be baby-sitters?" His argument was clever, but she didn't buy it.

Consequently, those egg babies got shoved into a shoebox, crammed into his backpack, and carried around with him for the better part of two days in an effort to salvage his grade.

"Egg kids are a real pain," he grumbled quite often. "You can't just dump them somewhere. You've got to drag them with you wherever you go!"

"I know the feeling," I empathized sarcastically. "Wait 'til you have to feed them, make them clean up their rooms, and be sure they get their homework done," I added as I rolled my eyes. My son was thrilled when Thursday rolled around. Joyfully, he turned his egg kids back in. (One had cracked its skull somehow in the shoebox. Fortunately, they were hard-boiled.) Somehow he managed to survive the assignment, and I think he might have learned a thing or two in the process.

I considered trying to explain to him how he really would have gotten used to his egg babies if he had let them hang around a little longer; how taking care of them could have actually brought him joy; how his "children" could have become a vital and fun part of his life; and how one day he might actually consider them a tremendous blessing—but I knew he wasn't ready to understand.

So I explained it all to the cat. He might not be a good sitter, but he's a great listener.

Know When to Say No, Part 2

Helen Widger Middlebrooke

I should have said no—again.

It wasn't the time for a haircut. It was after 10 P.M.—it was time for bed. Especially for a tired mother who had been operating all day long on four hours' sleep. But he begged.

"I'm tired," I said. "I don't feel like cutting hair." He begged more.

"I need to go to bed." He got out the clippers, scissors, and drape.

"I didn't say I was going to do it." He sat down.

"You remember the camp two years ago?"

Yes, he remembered the day the clipper guide broke in the middle of a buzz cut. He went to camp with a new hat, which hid a very prominent patch of fuzz.

Yet he continued pleading. He had to have a buzz cut. His

hair was too long, too hot. Clearly, he was desperate. And I was too tired to fight.

So it was that I plugged in the clippers, secured the broken guide with my finger, and began shearing his thick red mop.

Buzzzzz. Up the back. *Buzzzzz.* Up the left side. *Buzzzzz.* Up the right side.

All that was left was a Mohawk-like strip on top. "I think I'll stop there. See what you think."

He thought it was kind of "cool" and threatened to keep it. But he came back to have the job finished.

On top of his head was a near-bald patch. I dropped the clippers and began to cry.

BUZ—the clippers caught a knot! My finger slipped! The guide came off. And—

"Noo!!! I did it again!!!"

On top of his head was a near-bald patch. I dropped the clippers and began to cry. He ran to a mirror, and to my amazement, laughed.

When the emotions subsided, I turned the buzz cut into a fuzz cut. I wanted to say, "You should have learned from history." Instead I just apologized over and over.

"It's okay, Mom," he reassured me. "I shouldn't have pushed you to do it when you were tired. It looks okay."

It certainly does.

Especially beneath his new hat.

> *My children do not always learn from history,*
> *and neither do I.*
> *Let me not be so proud as to think that*

anything I do is new or grand,
for there is nothing new under the sun.
Let me not think that I can do anything without You.
And those times that I fall,
let me know You are always the same,
always loving and forgiving,
and ever willing to give me another chance.

funny honeys

♡ ♡ ♡ ♡ ♡
The Miracle of Creation

One night a wife found her husband standing over their baby's crib. As he stood looking down at the sleeping infant, she saw on his face a mixture of emotions: disbelief, doubt, delight, amazement, enchantment, skepticism.

"A penny for your thoughts," she said.

"It's amazing!" he replied. "I just can't see how anybody can make a crib like that for only $46.50."

—Bob Phillips, Bob Phillips Encyclopedia of Good Clean Jokes

23 Ways to Amuse Yourself during the Football Season

Lynn Bowen Walker

For some reason I've had an aversion to football season ever since I was in labor and my husband begged to wheel the hospital's television set into the delivery room so he wouldn't miss highlights from the NFL Game of the Week.

But I'm over it now. I'm a firm believer in water under the bridge, let bygones be bygones, and there's not much a few dozen bouquets of flowers won't fix.

Also, and I heard this once from a halftime commentator, the best defense is a good offense. I have no idea what that means. But that doesn't change the fact that I did need to formulate a plan in order to make it through the Autumn blight of pre-season, mid-season, and post-season games with my good humor intact. So here it is. My plan.

For all of us remote-control widows: We can endure with grace this season that swallows our man's attention from back-to-school-

shopping-days through New Year's, simply by choosing a few of the following ideas to try while the love of our life sits nearby, mesmerized by clumps of little men swarming over other little men in vain attempts to locate which little man actually holds the very little ball. With our game plan in mind, we can settle back for the most viewing pleasure we've had since the power failed during that bowl game back in '97.

See you at halftime.

- Write a contract where the "signee" promises to clean all toilet bowls for one year. Wait for a particularly intense play, then slide it over for your mate to sign.

- Wear old clothes, brandish a wrench, and announce you are going outside to work on the brakes of his car.

- Give yourself a home perm and plant yourself close to him. Make sure it's the stinky kind.

- Challenge him during commercials to try working the remote with his toes.

- Ask who is playing. Wait two minutes. Ask what color their "outfits" are. Wait two minutes. Ask who you should root for. Wait two minutes. Ask how you can tell when points are scored. Shrug your shoulders and smile cutely.

- Install yourself and a jigsaw puzzle at a card table right next to the TV set. Exclaim loudly at each piece that fits.

- Bring him a drink and put it just out of reach.

- Fashion hamburgers into the shape of a football. With carrot sticks as goal posts practice your forward pass.

- Cut confetti and throw it on yourself.

- Practice French braiding the hair on your dog's tail. Practice French braiding the hair on your husband's legs. But skip the big red bow; guys hate that.

- Practice speaking as fast as you can for 60-second intervals. This is a practical skill.

- Practice self-control as he informs you this is only the first of three games today. See if you remember your Lamaze breathing techniques.

- Run the vacuum. "Accidentally" trip on the television power cord, pulling it out of the socket.

- Discuss world politics with the tropical fish.

- Make his favorite cookies. Leave them in the kitchen. Time him as he hurtles toward the cookies between plays.

- Snap pictures of him in various television-watching poses. Take enough to fill an album. Present it to him on his next birthday.

- Massage his ears.

- Insist that there's a great love story playing on Channel 36. Bargain for dinner at Chez Francais in exchange for your returning the remote control.

- Fiddle with the knobs on his CD player. Try to locate a station that plays opera. Turn the volume to high.

- Count his gray hairs. Report how many he has. Pluck them out.

- Calculate how many calories you can burn by shuttling trays of food from the kitchen to the TV room. Slip some pulverized cauliflower into the bean dip and see if he notices.

- Model your newest lingerie at halftime. Sing Boogie Woogie Bugle Boy at the top of your lungs, but only if you can carry a tune.

- Have a baby. Hold firm on your refusal to let him wheel the television set into the delivery room, however. With all you're going through, viewing you instead of the Gatorade Bowl is the least he can do.

Forget Marriage Seminars—
Try Wallpapering

Sharon Colwell

Everything I needed to know about my marriage I learned by wallpapering with my husband. Romantic weekend getaways are wonderful and marriage seminars and books are helpful, but I dare any married couple to try wallpapering together—that'll show you what your marriage is really made of.

Twenty years ago Tom and I had just moved into our first house, an older city bungalow with a lot of "character." It wasn't a dream house, but it wasn't a nightmare either. With a little work, we knew it would be destined for greatness.

On a beautiful Saturday morning in September, we decided to create a work of art out of our living room. We had picked a miniprint wallpaper made of sturdy vinyl—to hide any cracks in the walls—just right for our classic, aged, character-ridden living room. After breakfast we dressed in our new painter's overalls and set up a table in the middle of the room. Then Tom began the

serious work of assembling his tools: plumb line, chalk, ruler, T-square, razor knife, scissors, powdered wallpaper paste, water, stirrer, bucket, sponge, rags, brushes, and roller. By 10:30, two hours into the job, we were ready to hang some wallpaper.

Tom took on the manly job of measuring, marking, and dropping the plumb line. Since I had had considerable experience making peanut butter sandwiches, I was given the job of wallpaper paste spreader. Our house had elegant nine-foot ceilings, so it took awhile for me to cover the entire first wallpaper strip with paste. I hadn't figured that the strip would be longer than our worktable. As I neared the end of the strip, the other end began to curl up on itself, getting paste on the front side of the paper—as well as on the carpeting. No matter, we had taken the saleslady's advice and purchased that funny-looking natural sponge for clean up. Tom took a few minutes to line the floor under the table with newspapers, as I finished the first strip. All was going well—except that now the newspapers protecting the floor were sticking to the wallpaper.

By lunchtime, I had one strip thoroughly pasted and ready to hang. I struggled to pick up one end; I had no idea it would be so heavy. It took both of us to drag it off the table. Tom grabbed the top end and, holding it close to his body, climbed the ladder. I stood next to the ladder, feeding him the rest of the strip, with the front side of the heavy wallpaper draped over my head. Tom positioned it appropriately on the wall, pressed it down, and we decided to break for lunch.

At this point, we realized that the job was going to take a little longer than planned. To stop his goal-directed self from getting upset by this, my husband decided to lighten the mood. When we were dating, he had always liked it when my hair got

messy and curly from the humidity. Now he laughed and ran his hands through my pasty hair. And there was something weirdly romantic about the sticky kisses that followed. But then I spotted the drooping strip of wallpaper. It looked like a baggy-faced basset hound, with the paper bulging, rippling, and sagging like wrinkled skin.

"Catch it before it falls!" I shouted. We flung ourselves against the wall, saving our work. We edged it upward until it was nearly back in place. "Too much paste!" said Tom. The saleslady had told us to use the stiff brush to make the paper adhere to the wall, so he began the rescue effort. Using the foot-long brush, Tom smoothed the wallpaper flat in broad strokes. Paste kept oozing out from the edges, and I kept using the sponge to wipe it up. It seemed an hour until the paper was finally smooth.

That weekend we got three strips in place. By late October, five weeks into the project, we had finished only one wall. By November, we felt as if we had been wallpapering for an eternity. Is this what they do all day in hell?

Drudgery awaited us every Saturday. We missed going out with our friends. We had turned down a young couples fall retreat, where we had looked forward to good fellowship, hiking, volleyball, and lounging around the lodge. We realized how we longed for simple weekend pleasures like concerts, sporting events, and taking our daughter to the zoo. When people asked us about our weekend plans, we groaned and complained. Then they just stopped asking. Our friends became more and more distant as we saw our social life wither and die.

Tom and I found it hard not to glare at each other when we thought of another weekend of wallpapering. We began watching late-night TV on Fridays because we dreaded the inevitable

Saturday morning task. Then, we'd put off wallpapering until 2:00 P.M. Saturday. The project grew in length. The end of our labor seemed painfully out of reach.

One Friday night I lay awake thinking of strategies for finishing the project. Maybe we could leave the room half-papered and paint the remaining walls for a paint-and-paper decorating scheme. Maybe we could just pull off the strips we had pasted and paint the whole thing. Whose idea was it to wallpaper anyway? I was beginning to think maybe I didn't even like the pattern anymore.

Next morning, I proposed the idea to Tom. "How about if we can the whole thing? Just paint the walls. No more pasting, no more cooped-up Saturdays. Freedom!"

"How about we go out to breakfast." He suggested.

"But what about getting the walls done? I want this settled! Finished! Done! If we can't do it, maybe we need professional help!" I was surprised by the angry tears welling in my eyes. At that point, Tom mocked, "You need professional help!" I became enraged. I knew the kind of professional help he was thinking about. But he was right. We had gotten to the point where we'd better do something soon before we needed a professional marriage counselor's help.

"Okay. Let's eat out. We've got to talk about this." Our daughter went to grandma's, and we went to breakfast. Over eggs and toast, we agreed on two things: we both wanted to complete the task and to enjoy the process. So far, we hadn't been doing too well on either one. On our way home, we bought a new album by one of our favorite Christian singers. That afternoon, we invited our friends, Bill and Monica, to come for coffee, hear

the album, and see our partially finished walls. They encouraged us, prayed with us, and congratulated us on our progress. Like Nehemiah restoring the walls surrounding Jerusalem, Tom had taken on a monumental task, Bill said.

On the following Saturdays, I began calling Tom "my Nehemiah." Then he would climb the ladder, and with mock seriousness, announce to the family, "I am doing a great work, so that I cannot come down: why should the work cease, whilst I leave it, and come down to you?" I admired his new dedication. As we resumed our wallpapering task, we kept the new album playing, singing and brushing paste in time to the music. The work seemed to go faster now. When we finished a strip, we celebrated, dancing around the living room together, laughing and smearing paste on each other. We were beginning to enjoy the process.

Christmas arrived, and we finished the wall. It only took us four months. To celebrate, we had a huge holiday brunch that year with the extended family. The wall was done. We did it.

Most of all, during all those days Tom and I had accomplished something together that would outlast the wall. Our marriage had permanently bonded. Like many marriages, our wallpapering had started out as an adventure but had become drudgery. But by learning to talk things through, to be patient, and to work as a team, we found that the fun and enjoyment returned.

Wallpapering had taught us to celebrate the process as well as the completion. And we became as glued to each other as that wall and paper, ready for whatever really big challenges were ahead.

Fixin' Stuff

Becky Freeman

After a long day of playing handyman around the house, Scott plopped his tired body down in the old green rocker in my office. Ever since he was a little boy, Scott has been "fixin' stuff." And only the Lord can help the woman who even so much as suggests he might hire a professional. Fixin' stuff is my man's sacred territory, his boyish realm of "I can do it myself."

For a few seconds, Scott just sat and rocked, grateful for a respite as I finished up some editing. I typed in the last correction, swiveled my chair around, and propped my feet up on my husband's weary knees.

"Tired?" I asked.

"Exhausted," he answered, staring blankly ahead.

"So now that you are here, I suppose you'd better go ahead and tell me the news. Do we have water? And if we do, is it hot,

cold, or lukewarm? And I'm almost afraid to ask but…" I gazed upward at this point, my hands folded together. "Lord, have mercy on us, do we have a clothes dryer yet?" I crossed my fingers and shut my eyes tightly as I waited in suspense for the reply.

I should explain that for three weeks now, we've been without a clothes dryer. Actually we've always been without a legitimate clothes dryer. I bought the machine used—well used—from a local Laundromat for the bargain price of $20. For our 20 big ones, we got a harvest-gold machine that looked and sounded more like a giant rock tumbler than a clothes dryer. But these are the things you put up with when you are raising four kids on a tight budget.

In the beginning the dryer sounded as if it were tossing about a few small pebbles. Then it went through a period of time when the pebble-tumbling noises actually came to a halt, which would have been a relief except that our mechanically deranged appliance had other tricks up its belt. At that point our clothes tumbler went from merely drying our clothes to baking them. Honestly. White dress shirts began popping out of the steel door the color of perfectly browned toast. During this awkward stage of dryerhood, our clothes always smelled like they'd been dried at the end of a coat hanger over a campfire.

Finally Scott figured out how to adjust the temperature from bake/broil to normal, but then the rock-tumbling noises returned. Only this time the sound had graduated from mere namby-pamby pebble bumping to serious boulder grinding. We knew the dryer's days were numbered when Jim Ed, our next-door neighbor, came over and asked Scott if we could hear the horrible noise our "air conditioner" was making outside. Scott

had to confess that the ruckus Jim Ed had been hearing was not emitting from an outside AC unit, but from inside our laundry room's clothes dryer. I was sure it would blow at any moment, but for several more weeks it noisily, but efficiently, managed to keep our clothes dry. Finally, however, the hunk of metal clanked to a grinding halt. But, hey, we figured we'd certainly milked our 20 bucks out of it.

You may not believe this, but we actually had already purchased a nice, almost-new dryer. It was sitting on the back porch waiting for the old machine to give up the ghost so it could move in on its territory. "Why in the world," you might be wondering, "did we wait so long to replace Old Yeller?"

"Becky," he confessed in a tone that sounded near surrender, "I think I've had my fill of fixing stuff."

I'll tell you why. Because the new, improved dryer runs on propane. And before we could install it, for reasons only a husband can understand, we would have to let our butane tank temporarily run out of fuel. Why? So he could move the tank over to the side of the house. *Oh.* And if he were going to move the butane tank over to the side of the house, he would also need to go ahead and move the water tank from the bathroom to the laundry room. I hope this is making sense to you. And if he had to do that, well then, all sorts of plumbing lines and gizmos and connectors and such would have to be moved and welded and soldered and piped. "This could take days," Scott had been ominously predicting. Faced with this scenario, I agreed with my husband that the most logical thing to do under the circumstances was to stall as long as humanly possible.

This weekend however, with the expiring of the old dryer, the jig was up.

For the last four days, in addition to air-drying our laundry on the back porch like a family of hillbillies, we've also been coping without benefit of hot water—in January.

Over this weekend I've not seen either of Scott's hands without tools attached to them, and I've only caught brief glimpses of his face from behind bars and under pipes. He's grown the scraggly beginnings of a beard. His eyes have taken on a hollow, haunted look, and all his attempts at conversation have started with, "Becky, please tell me you've seen a little piece of metal that looks like an elbow" or "a donut" or "your grandfather's nose."

"Becky," he confessed in a tone that sounded near surrender, "I think I've had my fill of fixing stuff now."

"Do you want me to hire a—"

"Don't say it! Don't even *think* it. Give me time. I'll get my second wind."

And me? Oh, I've been pressing bravely on. I've devised an ingenious system, I think, for still managing to get my daily hot bath. I can go without almost anything, but anyone who knows me well knows I will not be deprived of my daily hot soak in the tub if I can help it. My system?

First I begin by putting four of my biggest pots on the stovetop to boil (we have an electric stove, thank goodness), and I heat one big bowl of water in the microwave.

Then I take off all my clothes (so as not to waste precious seconds when the stage is set), wrap a towel around me, and shuffle back and forth from the kitchen to the bathroom until I've emptied three gallons of boiling water into the bathtub. (Of course this has attracted a bit of attention from my children's visiting friends. "Hey, what's your mom cookin' in the bathroom? Does she always wear a towel when she boils water?")

Then I refill the pots, set them all back on the stove to boil again and jump into the tub before the water cools off. Midway through my bath, when my hair is all lathered up with shampoo, I pop out of the tub to repeat the running back and forth with hot pads and pots of boiling water in order to reheat the two inches of bathwater that have begun to cool.

See? Nothin' to it.

So now you understand how much I had vested in the answers I was about to receive from my bone-weary, handy husband. The news was mixed.

"Becky," he began solemnly, like Colin Powell at a military briefing, "as it now lines up, yes, we have a working clothes dryer."

"Hallelujah!"

"Yes, there is hot and cold running water in the bathtub."

"Oh, Baby, I knew you could do it!"

"However, there is no water at all in any of the bathroom sinks."

"Yuuuuuck…"

"In the kitchen I have hot water only coming out of the faucet."

"That I can live with."

"No water to the dishwasher."

"That I cannot. What about the washing machine?"

"Cold only."

"All in all, Sir," I replied with a dutiful salute, "not too shabby. The troops will survive. For a couple of days. But I cannot write

another word tonight. May I be dismissed to my appointment with a tub of steaming hot water?"

The Following Day

It was rather amusing this morning to watch the kids fighting over who got to use the bathroom first—to brush their teeth and wet their combs. I went to the kitchen sink for a cold drink of water and forgot that today's option from that particular source was limited to hot liquids only. Resigned, I put a tea bag in a cup of steaming water from the hydrant. As it was steeping, I glanced out the kitchen window when, what to my wondering eyes should appear—but a white commode on the lawn. Surely not…

I walked straight out the door in my morning robe and sure enough, there in front of God and the neighbors and everybody sat a porcelain potty.

> There in front of God and the neighbors and everybody sat a porcelain potty.

I did a quick about face and marched back in the house.

"Look, Scott," I stated in no uncertain terms, "I'm a very patient woman. I'm okay with table saws and towers of pink insulation stacked on my front porch. I can even handle a dryer on the back porch. But I draw the line at a lawn potty!"

"Gee, Beck," Scott answered calmly, sounding strangely like the character Tim on *Home Improvement*. "I just needed to spray it off. No need to get upset."

"Yeah, well, it's my potty and I'll cry if I want to!"

One look at my face and Scott knew I meant business. I'd reached my fix-it-man limit. As the kids and I loaded up the station

wagon for the drive to their school, I saw Scott run out the front door (in nothing but his boxer shorts), pick up the commode, and drag it to the front porch. Then he threw a blanket over it for camouflage.

I looked helplessly at the kids.

Zeke couldn't resist. He rolled down the window and shouted, "Hey, Dad, try putting a hat on it!"

Rachel followed up with, "And a carrot nose and a corncob pipe might look nice!"

Scott snickered and darted back into the house. I just shook my head.

He is taking off a few days to work on the house and get it in shape for a Friday-night pizza party for the kids' youth group. Hopefully, all our faucets will be running hot and cold again by then. (If not, it is safe to assume my blood will be.)

man-oh-man: laughing with the guys we love

Too Hot to Handle

The bride and groom moved from the altar up to the unity candle on the platform. The pastor then explained to the audience that the blowing out of the two outer candles represented the couple's surrendering their individual freedom. The groom whispered back to the pastor, "Would it be all right if we just blow out her candle?"

—STAN TOLER, THE YEAR-ROUND BOOK
OF SERMON IDEAS, STORIES, AND QUOTES

Little Henry Sounds Off

Dan N. "Max" Mayhew

The trouble with taking the kids to church is they have to learn a whole new set of behavioral objectives. (For readers who may not be up on the lingo, a behavioral objective is a thing you want your kids to be able to *actually do* after you have taught them something. For example, you teach your second grader that worms are "yucky" so that he won't bring several home in his pants pocket as pets then forget they are there until after the pants have gone through a complete cycle in the new washer.) A behavioral objective—B.O. for short—can be plenty complicated at home and at school, but at church it is often incomprehensible.

Parents are at a disadvantage when teaching kids how to behave in church because they are unable to talk above a whisper. The average preschooler, on the other hand, has yet to grasp the concept of talking quietly, much less "whispering." Further

complicating the issue is the fact that whispering is one of the BO's of church life. The result is that even if the child forgets to whisper, Mom and Dad are forced to. This leaves them without one of their most formidable weapons: the "parental authority voice." This way of talking is about an octave lower than normal and is calculated to convince the child that Mommy means business, or Daddy is in complete control of the situation. Under normal conditions the conversation would go like this:

> *Little Henry is squatting next to a worm the size of a loaf of French bread.*
> *MOMMY: Don't touch the worm. It's yucky.*
> *Little Henry shows no signs of having heard. His chubby little hand is inches away from the worm and getting closer...*
> *MOMMY (using her parental authority voice): YEECHHH, Henry! Don't touch that!*

In church, though, use of the parental authority voice is severely limited. In a whisper it sounds like somebody is strangling a muppet. Worse, it is often too late...

> *The opening hymn is finished. The minister steps to the pulpit and invites the congregation to sit down. The sanctuary rustles to an orderly quiet. Then little Henry, having studied the profile of a man across the aisle, loudly announces, "Daddy, look! That man's tummy hangs out!"*

At this point, the time for remedial action is past. There is no time for the parental authority voice. Limited by the environment, Daddy is forced to resort to the "parental desperation response" which sounds like, "SHHHHHHHHHHHHHH!!!!!!" Unfortunately, to be effective, "shhhhhshing" has to be nearly as

loud as little Henry's original announcement, which defeats the whole purpose of trying to get him to whisper in the first place. Furthermore, the parental "Shhhsh!!" is often accompanied by a hand hastily clamped over little Henry's mouth so he can't point out that the pastor has no hair. This can result in little Henry saying something like "OWWWWWWWW!" which is hardly the kind of exclamation you could expect a child (or an adult, for that matter) to whisper.

With practice, it is possible to train the kids to behave appropriately without having to actually talk to them. This usually is done through facial expression, which conveys that if the child persists in whatever he is doing he may well be riding home strapped to the trunk lid. My most effective facial weapon was the "jaw clench" while Judy perfected what the children, now full grown, refer to as "the eyebrow."

With practice, it is possible to train the kids to behave appropriately without having to actually talk to them.

Another behavioral objective in church relates to the proper response to the offering plate. The B.O. in response to a passed plate in church is different than in other settings. For example, while visiting your snootiest relative, you may sit in the living room where Aunt Bertie has set a plate of hors d'oeuvres. Little Molly has been carefully coached while still in the car, but you watch nervously as the plate is offered to her. What will little Molly do? Will she:

- grab a handful of whatever is on the plate and cram it into her chubby cheeks like a starving chipmunk and scatter crumbs all over the love seat?

- say, "Yuk!" and make a face that communicates that she could just as well be viewing road kill?

- politely say, "Thank you," and take one of whatever is on the plate.

- sweetly say, "No, thank you!"

While at Aunt Bertie's, if little Molly responds to the passing of the plate by doing either "c" or "d" Aunt Bertie will likely launch into raptures of laudatory bliss. While at church, doing any of the above will cause Mommy and Daddy to instantly appear several inches shorter and take refuge behind the nearest hymnal.

In addition to helping your child master the nuances of church behavior, you may also want to pay attention to their interpretation of what they learn there. One mom reported that her daughter was under the impression that King Solomon had 200 wives and 700 porcupines; and one dad was shocked to learn from his son that Samson had wiped out the Philippines with the ax of the apostles.

Of Things Green and Slimy

G. Ron Darbee

There I was, minding my own business, not hurting another soul in the world, about to take the first bite from my double-meat, double-cheese hamburger extravaganza when she stopped in front of our table. A well-meaning, good-natured busybody—self-appointed patrol officer for the cholesterol police, she felt moved to share her philosophy with me.

"Do you know what you're doing to your body?" she asked. She looked at me with that same you-should-be-ashamed-of-yourself look my mother always saved for report cards and conversations with the youth pastor.

"Nourishing," I answered. "Yes, I believe that's the term, Ma'am. I'm nourishing my body."

"You most certainly are not!" she lectured. "You're killing yourself, that's what you're doing."

Sue isn't very helpful in these situations, choosing to ignore

rather than confront people who freely express their opinions. But alas, such is not the way of men.

"If it would make you feel any better, I could lie down right here in the booth and you can drive a steak through my heart— rare if you please, with lots of fat." My comment, intended to amuse, neither entertained nor discouraged our health-minded visitor.

"Well, if you're not concerned for your health," she continued, "or the well-being of your family," she motioned toward the kids who appeared to be enjoying the conversation, "you could at least show some respect for God's creation."

Finally, a topic I felt qualified to discuss. "Run that by me again, Ma'am, that part about God's creation."

"Every time you eat a hamburger, you kill one of God's creatures," she said. The woman obviously didn't understand how many hamburgers come from the average beef cow.

"I was under the impression God placed animals on earth for man's use," I said. "He expects us to eat them. That's why cows are so dumb and slow. Otherwise they'd be real mean and fast. I imagine that would make them considerably more difficult to milk, now that I think about it."

Persistence not a quality the woman lacked, she refused my attempt to divert her into a whimsical discussion on cattle temperament and held firmly to the original line of questioning. "With all the variety nature offers, why must you insist on eating beef?"

"Oh, I don't know, Ma'am," I said, beginning to tire with the verbal exchange. "I guess because I can't afford veal."

"I hope you choke on that hamburger," she said and stormed away from our table.

"So much for loving God's creation," I said to Sue as the woman drifted into the distance.

"That wasn't very nice," Sue said, amidst the cheers of "Good one, Dad," from Ron and Melissa.

"Tell me about it," I said. "Some nerve, accosting a family trying to enjoy a simple meal."

"I'm talking about you."

"Me?!" I said, completely unaware of my transgression. "What did I do?"

"You were rude and aggressive, that's what," she said. "Couldn't you just smile and ignore her, instead of engaging in a battle of wits?" After all these years, you'd think Sue could answer that one on her own.

"I'm sorry, Sweetheart," I said. "I realize that wasn't the best example for the kids." The next few minutes were dedicated to explaining to Ron and Melissa alternate ways of dealing with such people.

"You know something, Sue," I said as we were driving home that evening. "Something just dawned on me. That woman in the restaurant tipped the scales in excess of two hundred pounds, if I'm any judge of size. And I'm not making fun of her, but she didn't get that big on a diet of snow peas and granola. There's got to be some serious animal by-products involved in that equation."

"Maybe that's why she was so adamant," Sue said. "It could be she's battling a health or weight problem and wanted to save you from suffering too." That's one of the things I love most about my wife; she really does try to see the best in all people.

Mistakenly, I thought we shared the last words on that subject, but consequences associated with the lovely woman's tirade surfaced a few days later.

"I saw an article in today's paper that I want you t read," Sue said when I arrived home from work. "It's about the effects of cholesterol and high-fat foods in our diets."

"Let me guess, they're against it," I said.

"I'm not kidding," Sue said. "You should read this." She handed me a clipping from the "lifestyles" section. "We might want to think about changing our eating habits."

"I don't want to change my eating habits, Sue," I said. "Eating tofu and bean sprouts doesn't make you live any longer, it just *seems* longer. Every meal is like an eternity."

"This isn't a joke. We're talking about our health."

"No, you are talking about our health, Sue. I'm just trying to figure out the sudden urgency of a low-fat diet."

"Well, I borrowed a couple of cookbooks from the library," Sue said, "and as long as I'm the one cooking, we're going to try to eat better."

Her ability to negotiate from a position of power was, at that moment, not one of the other things I loved most about my wife. The cookbooks she brought home included: *101 Ways to Prepare Zucchini, Bean Curd, Your Heart's Best Friend,* and *Out of the Frying Pan,* a guide to boiled dinners. Somewhere a deep-dish pizza called my name.

The evening's dinner verified that there was in fact 101 ways to prepare zucchini. What the author failed to mention, however, is that there are only three ways to prepare your family to eat it. They are: Bribery—"If you eat your zucchini you can have some dessert"; Blackmail—"If you don't finish every bite, you'll find it on your breakfast plate in the morning"; and Brute Force—"Eat the zucchini right this minute or else!"

Finishing every last piece of the green, slimy vegetable as an

example to our children, I tried to cover the gagging sounds that emanated with each mouthful. Mistaking my good example for approval, Sue offered to send the leftovers for my next day's lunch.

"That won't be necessary, Sue," I said. "I think I'll stop by the cafeteria and grab a salad." (I neglected to mention my salad would be served on a bun and crowned with a quarter-pound of beef.) "What's on the menu for tomorrow's night?" I asked.

"Meatloaf surprise," she answered.

I started to salivate at the thought of a juicy, cholesterol-infested meat loaf. "What's the surprise part?" I asked cautiously.

"No meat. You mix two pounds of tofu with the same spices you normally put in meat loaf and cook it in a mold. The cookbook claims you won't be able to tell the difference."

"Don't bet on it," I said.

For two weeks, not an animal carcass graced our kitchen, and the children began to exhibit signs of rebellion. "I want a pizza, Dad!" Ron said while we hid in his room and shared a contraband beef jerky left over from his last camping trip. "And I don't care what I have to do to get it."

"Give it some time, Son," I said. "A couple more weeks and your mother will snap out of it. I've seen this sort of thing before."

"I don't think we have a couple of weeks, Dad. I'm starting to dream about French fries. If you don't do something, I'm going to run away and join a fast-food chain."

"Which one?" I asked, wondering if I might join him.

Melissa knocked softly on the door and begged to come in. "I know you guys are hiding something in there," she said. "Let me in, and I won't tell Mom. I just want a tiny piece."

"You don't even know what it is!" Ron whispered through the door. "Go away!"

"I don't care what it is, but I want some," she returned. "I mean it! I'll tell Mom." Ron let his sister enter and grudgingly turned over a small portion of our bounty. Melissa devoured the jerky like a hungry wolf.

"So this is what we've come to," I said, cleaning the remnants of jerky from between my teeth. "Hiding in Ron's room and sneaking food. I never though I'd eat anything we found in your room, Son. I promise to talk to your mother. We'll get this thing resolved before the dog becomes endangered. I don't want to come home and find Rascal on the barbecue."

Spending a few hours of vacation time, I came home early the next day to reason with Sue before the children got out of school. A wonderful and familiar smell greeted me as I entered the front door.

"You're home early!" Sue said, surprised at my arrival. "I didn't expect you so soon." Her words were laced with guilt and a hint of Worcestershire.

"What do you have on that plate behind you, Sue?"

"This plate? Oh, nothing really. It's just an itsy-bitsy, teeny-weeny slab of meat. I couldn't help myself."

"And so ends the not-so-great health experiment," I said. "Welcome back to the world of carnivorous dining, Sweetheart. What's for supper?"

"I don't want to go back to eating the way we did," she said. "We should be careful."

"Careful is fine," I said. "Good things in moderation. But no more trying to maintain life on rabbit food and birdseed. Now, what do you want for supper? I'll spring for take-out."

We agreed on pizza, everything but anchovies. Meat, dairy, vegetable, and bread—the four basic food groups. It is possible to compromise and still eat well. A meal never tasted so good.

Pop Quiz

Phil Callaway

Please answer each question honestly, bearing in mind that while it is impossible to fail this test, your answers may determine where you'll spend the night.

1. When you are wrong, you will admit it to your partner:
   A. Within seconds.
   B. Just as soon as cows produce root beer.
   C. Usually before sunset.

2. On your most recent vacation, you:
   A. Strolled sun-soaked beaches barefoot, then basked in the glow of each other's eyes.
   B. Left messages on each other's answering machines.
   C. Had to come home for a rest.

3. Which of the following most accurately describes the frequency of your lovemaking?
   A. Tri-weekly
   B. Try weakly
   C. Try weekly

4. Complete this sentence: I believe the Children of Israel wandered in the wilderness for 40 years because:
   A. God was testing their marriages.
   B. Moses didn't pay attention when his wife was giving directions.
   C. Moses wanted everybody to appreciate the Promised Land once they got there.

5. When you're watching TV together, who controls the remote?
   A. We do not watch television; we go for walks and talk about our feelings.
   B. I do.
   C. Whoever gets it first.

6. The food that best sums up your spouse's kiss:
   A. Red-hot chili peppers
   B. Airline omelet
   C. Hot apple pie

7. The movie title that best sums up your sex life:
   A. Some Like it Hot
   B. Gone with the Wind
   C. As Good as It Gets

8. (For men only) You've just bought a late-model minivan, complete with CD player. The phone rings. It's your frenzied wife calling from Biff's Auto Repair to tell you she has totaled the van. You:

   A. Ask if she's okay.

   B. Total the telephone.

   C. Ask if she's okay—and if the CD player still works.

9. (For women only) After a particularly tough day, your husband has crashed in front of the TV set. You decide to:

   A. Stand beside the TV set and try on lingerie.

   B. Put fiberglass insulation in his pajamas.

   C. Pour two tall ginger ales and crash with him.

10. Your definition of communication is:

    A. I am attentive to my partner's communication needs. I listen well and share openly my thoughts, aspirations, and feelings.

    B. Nintendo.

    C. Sorry, I was distracted. Could you repeat the question?

11. It's 12:30 A.M. and neither of you can sleep. Your spouse says, "Honey, I'm hungry. Would you get me a slice of cheese?" You say:

    A. "Is that all, sweetheart? How about a salad with croutons?"

    B. "Zzzzzz."

    C. "Swiss or cheddar?"

How to score:

If you answered "A" more than six times, thanks for taking this quiz during your honeymoon. We wish you all the best in the years ahead. If you found yourself gravitating to the "B" responses, take an aspirin and resubscribe to *Marriage Partnership* in the morning. Also—find a soft pillow. You'll need it on the couch.

If you chose "C" five or more times, you've got a good thing going. Collect 10 bonus points if you also answered "A" more than once. Sounds like some flexibility, lots of laughter, and a servant heart are keeping your marriage fresh.

Now, break out the ginger ale. It's time to try weekly!

what do women and cheese
have in common?
we both age well

Really Digging His Wife

An archaeologist is the best husband any woman can have. The older she gets, the more interested he is in her.

—Bob Phillips,
Over the Hill and on a Roll

Playing Connect-the-Dots with My Age Spots

Laura Jensen Walker

When I was young, I thought age spots only appeared on "older" people—say in their seventies and eighties.

Although what constitutes "older" has now changed a bit.

Middle age has definitely moved up to the higher end of the scale.

Now 60 is middle-aged. Hey, I've heard of people living to 120. It can happen.

I remember seeing age spots on my grandparents and figuring it was just a natural part of growing old—something I wouldn't have to worry about for years and years.

That's why it was such a shock when they first appeared on my chest.

Since I'm a breast cancer survivor, I always pay special attention to any changes in my chest area, so when these pale brown dots

suddenly appeared, I grew concerned and made an appointment to see my doctor.

"Those are just age spots, Laura," he told me with a gentle smile.

"AGE spots? But I'm barely forty!"

"Some people get them earlier than others."

Well, *that* was a great comfort.

On the way home from the doctor's, I stopped by the grocery store to drown my sorrows in some chocolate-chip ice cream.

Those brown spots I can handle.

But the ones on my chest really took some getting used to.

It wasn't as if there were just one or two stray marks either. There were about a baker's dozen sprinkled across my chest.

And when I connected them, they formed the great state of Texas.

Do you know the song "Deep in the Heart of Texas"? Then sing along with me.

> *The dots at night*
> *Are big and bright*
> *(clap-clap-clap-clap)*
> *Deep on the chest like Texas.*

I'm not the only one in my family with interesting spots. My cousin Susie, who's in her early fifties, recounts, "After observing my arms recently and noticing the masses of white spots where pigment had once been, my six-year-old granddaughter Ashley exclaimed, 'Wow, Grandma! Look at all those polka dots. Cool!'"

Hey—perhaps if Susie connected all her dots she could form California on her arm. And maybe if my relatives and I all joined together with our spots, we could form a jigsaw puzzle of the whole Western United States.

Top Ten Signs You're Growing More Mature

Stan Toler

10. Your teeth spend the night in a jar.
9. You have an executive "lift" chair.
8. It takes you longer to go to sleep than it did to get tired.
7. You and the pharmacist are on a first-name basis.
6. It takes you twice as long to look half as nice.
5. The pressing question of your life is, "Where did I park the car?"
4. You get winded playing Bible Trivia.
3. You know all the answers, but nobody asks you the questions.
2. You walk with your head held high…to see through your bifocals.
1. Shuffleboard doesn't sound too bad.

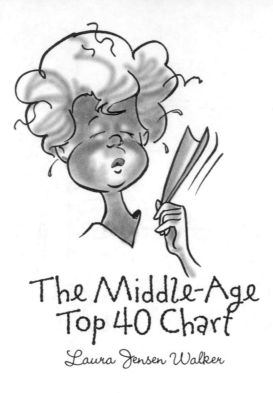

The Middle-Age Top 40 Chart

Laura Jensen Walker

Okay, now that you've reached middle age, it's important that you be able to identify all those exciting physical and mental changes you're going through.

That's why I've taken the time, dear reader, to compile this very scientific, thoroughly researched, and exhaustive list for you. Although, you might want to write it down so you don't forget it.

Very Scientific and Exhaustive List of Middle-Age Terms

1. Age Spots: Cute freckles gone bad.

2. Arm Flaps: Those under-the-upper-arm swings that can knock out a man, woman, or child from across the room. (First

spotted on the scary flying monkeys in *The Wizard of Oz.*)

3. Bifocals: What you wear so you can see all your brand-new facial hair. (Caution: May cause dizziness.)

4. Brain Fade: What mine is doing right now as I try to finish this book at 3:30 A.M.

5. Chin Hair: A continuous thread of conclusive aging (and yet another new place to pluck).

6. Crow's Feet: The tracks of my tears; whatever happened to that spring chicken?

7. Double Chin: The ultimate in rubber necking.

8. Dropped Derriere: When you can see your backside from the front.

9. The Drop Zone: The area of the body—from the eyelids to the kneecaps—where everything starts to go south for the winter…spring…summer.

10. Eye Lift: Expensive surgical procedure to give you that taut, youthful wide-eyed

look instead of Dean Martin's droop.

11. Fan: Essential weapon in the hot-flash war. No menopausal woman should ever leave home without it.

12. Fuddy-Duddy: You've turned into a fuddy-duddy when the only party you go to is Tupperware.

13. Gingko: Miracle supplement to help you remember why you opened the door of the refrigerator.

14. Gray Hair: On men it may look distinguished, but for women, it's something we try to extinguish.

15. HRT: (Hormone Replacement Therapy) AKA Hot Flash First Aid.

16. Hot Flash: Better than an I.D., this furnace blast from the waist up tells everyone around you that you're over forty.

17. Law of Forgetfulness: If it isn't written down, you'll forget it.

18. Menopause: The only time in your life when you get to have the same wardrobe from

season to season—all summer clothes (which means white after Labor Day, Mom).

19. Menopausal Mustache: Something every woman over forty can look forward to bleaching, plucking, or waxing.

20. Mentalpause: Inability to remember names, places, and what you were just about to say (AKA brain fade, or senior moment).

21. Middle Age: Caught between a glamour girl and a golden girl.

22. Middle-Age Spread: A tummy just waiting to be tucked.

23. Midlife Crisis: When your husband comes home one day astride a Harley or sporting a pierced eyebrow.

24. Mood Swings: Pick a mood, any mood, then change it in a heartbeat, add tears, and stir.

25. Mother-in-the-Mirror: Mirror, mirror on the wall. Instead of looking like Snow White, you're your mother after all.

26. Naps: Ecstasy.

27. Night Sweats: A good reason to shop the white sales.

28. Pencil Test: Important perky teen coming-of-age ritual along with SATs. After forty, do NOT attempt at home.

29. Perimenopause: The beginning of the end.

30. PMS: A walk in the park next to menopause.

31. Puffy Thighs: Forget cottage cheese thighs, we're talking mega-marshmallows here.

32. Reading Glasses: Also known as cheaters, now available at your local drugstore for only ten bucks.

33. Sex after Fifty: Huh? Did you say something, dear?

34. Thermostat Wars: He may get the remote, but you've won the real battle: supreme control of the thermostat.

35. Thinning Hair: A wig a day keeps the bald spot at bay.

36. Varicose Veins: Coast-to-coast road map permanently imprinted on your legs, complete with rivers, mountains, and railroad tracks.

37. Vitamins: What you have to take in order to keep having sex after fifty.

38. Warm Wave: Baby hot flash.

39. Whatchamacallit: Latest word addition to the middle-age dictionary—must be said in tandem with pointing at common, everyday object.

40. Wrinkle Cream: Save your money. Buy chocolate instead.

16

just when you
thought it was safe
to stop laughing

Happiness Concluded

A pastor received the following thank you note from a newlywed in his congregation: "Dear Pastor: I want to thank you for performing our marriage ceremony. It was beautiful the way you brought my happiness to a conclusion."

—PASTOR DENNIS R. FAKES,
MORE HOLY HUMOR

Security Blanket

Sheri Rose Shepherd

Whenever I hear a scary story, I become convinced that the same terrifying thing will happen to me at any minute. Is that the wind blowing, or is someone about to leap out of the bushes and conk me on the head? Common sense would suggest that I avoid listening to scary stories, but common sense doesn't always have the upper hand in life.

Not long ago, a friend told me about a scary incident at a gas station. The attendant came over to a customer's car window and the customer asked for a fill-up. The attendant filled her tank and went back to the window to get her credit card. Glancing in the backseat, he noticed a gunman hiding on the floor. The attendant went inside for a minute, then came back out and said, "Ma'am, your credit card isn't working, and you'll have to come into the office."

Naturally the woman was in a hurry. "Here, let me give you another card," she said.

"No, ma'am," he replied. "It's very important that you get out of the car and take this phone call from the credit card company. They absolutely insist on talking to you."

The young attendant had called the police, and as the woman picked up the phone, the police arrived and arrested the gunman. That young man probably saved her life.

After hearing this story, I had a severe case of the creeps and spent the rest of the afternoon checking the backseat of my car as I drove around. When I got home, my mother-in-law's van was on the street in front of our house. Steve was busy in the garage and asked if I would back the van into the driveway so we could load it up.

I had left the van in reverse, and it was backing across the grass directly toward the neighbors' living room window.

I hopped in, started the engine, and put the gearshift in reverse. Glancing in the rearview mirror, I thought I saw the shape of a man in the backseat. I didn't see his gun, but no doubt it was just behind the seat. Stricken with terror and seeing no gas station attendant nearby, I jumped out and started sprinting across the neighbors' front yard.

After running a few steps, I turned to see if the gunman was following me. He wasn't—but the van was. I had left it in reverse, and it was backing across the grass directly toward the neighbors' living room window. I ran like a maniac, grabbed the open door on the driver's side, and tried to use my tennis shoes as brakes.

At that moment, Steve looked up to see what all the commotion was about and saw me locked in mortal combat with a mini-

200

van headed for death and destruction. He dashed out of the house, jumped in through the passenger's side, and threw on the brakes just as I was beginning to plow through the front flower bed. We missed the front window by less than a foot.

Peeking into the backseat, I saw that my armed assailant was in fact an extremely lifelike blanket. It was an unforgettable lesson in how easy it is to overreact to scary stories about attacks that may never happen to me personally. I had allowed the gas station story to foster fear and carelessness. Focusing on my fear made me forget that my Protector is always beside me.

When Jesus' disciples were caught in an awful storm in the Sea of Galilee, their fear was heartstopping and it was real. But their fear was unfounded. Jesus was with them then just as he is with us now.

Enough real problems exist in the world, so there's no sense in making up our own.

Accidental Perspective
Patsy Clairmont

I bounded out the door, energized because I had completed a writing project and motivated by a purchase I was going to make. I had been working on a story for two days, and it had finally come together. While I was writing, in the back of my mind, I kept thinking about a used piece of furniture I had seen in town that would be just right for my office. I needed a book and display case, and this piece offered both, plus more. The price was right, too.

I was excited as I headed into our little town full of delightful shops offering wonderful "deals." I was almost to my destination when, in my rearview mirror, I noticed a car come up behind me at a fast clip. I remember thinking, *That guy is going to hit me if I don't scoot out of his way.* I added a little pressure to the gas pedal and turned my wheel to hurry into a parking space. That's when it happened. A loud thud was followed by crunching, scrunch-

ing, grinding sounds as my minivan rearranged the front fender of a parked car.

I am of the belief that if you're going to hit a vehicle, you should select one with someone inside. When you smack an empty, parked car, you pretty much rule out the chance the other person may have been at fault. All eyes are focused on you. Also, if you must have an obvious accident, it's better not to do it on Main Street in your hometown.

I jumped out of the van and ran over to look at the smooshed car. The victim's vehicle had two silver beauty marks streaking down the side, and the chrome fender curled out instead of in, giving it a flared appearance.

Then I ran inside an office and asked if the car belonged to anyone there. It didn't, so I headed for the next building, when I heard someone call my name.

A lady I had just met at Bible study two weeks prior waved and ran across the road in my direction. She gave me a hug and told me everyone in the ladies' dress shop heard me hit the car and came to the window to see what had happened and who had done it. When I stepped out of my van, she squealed and announced, "I know that woman!" In a small town, anonymity is difficult.

Then she added as she checked out the crumpled car, "You could tell this story at conferences."

Trust me—at this point, I was not eager to tell my husband, much less the world, what I had done.

I dashed into the shop where the bookcase was and called to the clerk, "I have to go turn myself in at the police station, but would you please measure the bookcase for me? I'll be right back to purchase it."

As I headed for the front door, I heard a sweet voice say, "I just sold it."

"No!" I exclaimed. "You don't understand! I hit a car in my attempt to get here and buy this piece" (as if that would make a difference). Then I whined, "The buyer wasn't driving a dark blue Buick, was she?"

The saleswoman assured me she wasn't. I could tell she felt bad about my situation, but I felt worse. On the way to the police station, I thought, *Maybe I'll have them throw me in the slammer and sleep off this trip to town.*

When I arrived, I confessed to a woman behind a barred glass window that I had committed a crime. She called for an officer to come and write a report. While I was waiting, I noticed the zipper on my pants was down and my red shirttail was sticking out like a road flag. I quickly turned away from the men sitting in the waiting area to "fix" myself and tried not to think about how long my red tail had been waving. A fleeting recollection of me looking like Wee Willie Winkie as I ran from one store to the next, trying to find the car's owner, darted through my head.

The officer appeared and began to ask questions. Near the end of the inquest, he asked, "How much damage did you do to your vehicle?"

"I don't know," I answered.

"You don't know?" he echoed.

"I don't know," I validated.

"Why don't you know?" he pushed.

"Because I didn't look."

"Why didn't you look?" he asked in disbelief.

"I'm in denial," I confessed.

"You have to look," he told me. Then he sent me out to get my registration.

I returned, paper in hand.

"Well," he said, "how much damage?"

"Sir, I didn't look," I said with polite resignation.

He shook his head and gave me back my registration. As I was leaving, I heard him say, "You'll have to look."

When I got home, I asked Les to go out and look.

It turned out I had swiped her car with my running board. The board wasn't off, yet it wasn't on.

It was neither here nor there but suspended in air. Threads at each end dangled the board precariously.

Afterward, I realized that when we spend too much time looking in our rearview mirrors, we may hit something right in front of us. Looking back is an important part of conscientious driving, but it's not the only safety precaution.

I confessed to a woman behind a barred glass window that I had committed a crime.

Likewise, it's important for us to benefit from our past, but we don't want to get so stuck staring at yesterday that we collide with today in a destructive way.

Unlike the situation with my van, I can't send Les to check my past and assess how much damage was done. That's my responsibility. As the officer said, "You'll have to look." But once I take care of what I can do to repair the past, I then need to drive on, benefiting from occasional rearview references and perspective.

True Grace

Susan Duke

Alone in the doctor's combination bathroom/dressing room, I stepped out of the blue cotton gown and flushed the toilet, simultaneously reaching for my clothes and pantyhose hanging just above it on a hook.

I watched helplessly as my pantyhose slipped into the toilet bowl, swirled around, and headed south with a horrifying gurgle! *Oh, no! What am I going to do?*

I panicked!

After dressing as quickly as humanly possible, I snatched up my purse, shut the door, and headed for the receptionist's desk. As I smiled faintly and wrote a check for services rendered, I couldn't help thinking…*Poor doctor, this visit could cost him more than it cost me! I hope I haven't messed up the plumbing.* Looking back, I realize I should have come clean, confessed all, and accepted the consequences. But, the problem with imperfect

moments is that they sneak up on us, take us by surprise, and before we know it, we've blown all semblance of dignity.

I've stood in crowds of influential people praying no one would notice I was wearing one navy and one black shoe. I've hugged strangers I mistook for friends. I've innocently checked out at Wal-Mart wearing a necklace I'd tried on with the tag in plain sight— realizing, once out the door, that I had gotten away with shoplifting! (Red faced, I walked back inside and handed over the merchandise. No arrest was made!)

I watched helplessly as my pantyhose slipped into the toilet bowl and headed south with a horrifying gurgle!

I've come to the conclusion that the only way I can achieve real dignity in this life is by accepting that my quest for a perfect life is not immune to imperfect situations. While I'm amazed at the rush of embarrassing situations I can easily recall, I'm more amazed that God has innately equipped me to overcome…with true grace.

It's the kind of grace that unites the common and the elite— the meek and the mighty.

Jesus, though perfect, understands what imperfect situations and the sting of humiliation feel like. But because he was willing to walk, crawl, and stumble up a steep hill called Calvary—and give his life for our imperfection—*true grace* was born.

Awkward? I certainly think so. Did he overcome? Yes, indeed. Was it worth it?

You and I are living proof.

17

kids: God's way
of making sure
we laugh—
especially at
ourselves

Juvenile PMS

When Gabe was in the first grade, he came home one day complaining about the boy who sat next to him in school. "Mom," he moaned, "this is the whiniest kid. I mean, nobody can do anything to make him happy! All he does is gripe, gripe, gripe—all day long! Really, he's got the worst case of PMS I've ever seen in a kid."

—BECKY FREEMAN, CHOCOLATE CHILI PEPPER LOVE

How to Speak "Kid"

Helen Widger Middlebrooke

One of my heart's deepest desires is to truly communicate with my children.

I want to know them; I want them to know me.

But that's easier said than done. And it's getting harder as the years go by.

At first I thought talking with a two year old was tough. But the truth is, it's really very simple. The first rule in talking with two year olds is that you can't talk with two year olds. You talk at and to them; rarely with them.

To survive the twos, all you need are patience, humor, and ten phrases: Yes. No. I love you. Because I said so. Go potty. Pick up your toys. Be nice. Don't touch. Get your finger out of your nose. It's bedtime.

By age three, my children usually can converse. But to

understand them, I must be a master of toddler trivia. I must know, for example, my three year old's sound substitutions. "Benzahmen's fweeping" means the baby is not awake. And when she says, "The eagle woke me up," I must know her big brother likes to pretend he's an eagle.

The optimum age for understanding is between five and nine. They know how to speak, their vocabularies are better, and they still believe me. It's a wonderful time. I talk, they listen, and vice versa.

After the tenth birthday, they develop selective deafness. I talk, but they don't hear me. (Unless I'm in the closet, talking long distance to Grandma about presents.) This condition worsens until adolescence when they become selectively dumb. I talk; they hear—sometimes; they respond—sometimes…maybe…if they feel like it.

The other day, my thirteen-year-old city boy looked as though he had been farming.

"You need a bath," I said.

He stared at me as if I were from Mars. Slowly, his lip began to quiver. And then—he talked!

"Awwww, Mom."

My heart began to flutter.

At last! We had communicated!

Even though I can't always
communicate with those around me,
I can communicate with You anytime, Father.
Forgive me for not always availing myself of
Your ever present ear.
Let me learn to pray without ceasing
and to listen to You without interrupting.

We Thought They Were Asleep Till They Said Amen

Sue Buchanan

It's funny that Jesus tells his disciples not to hinder the little children in their pursuit of him. He certainly must have thought children were able to understand what it meant to be touched by him or he wouldn't have made such a big deal about it. In the very next verse, it says he placed his hands on them. Perhaps he was telling us that children are capable of understanding much bigger concepts than we give them credit for.

Of course, Wayne and I thought *our children* were always way out there ahead when it came to understanding the big concepts. One of our favorite family stories took place when Dana was eighteen months old. She often visited her grandparents in Wisconsin where every day a siren blew to mark the noon hour. It was loud, and it terrified her and left her screaming. In order to soothe her and help her understand the need for such a loud noise, her preacher grandpa told her it was to let the children

know it was time to go home for lunch. He even suggested that Dana say the words, "Go home and get your lunch," each time the whistle blew, which she would do at the top of her little lungs, albeit with the fear of God written all over her face.

One Sunday, our entire family (this included Wayne, his mom, his sister and her family, me, my mother and brother) was packed into the second row of the church, listening to Dad Buchanan deliver his sermon. (He was pretty wound up that day if I remember correctly.) It was a breezy Wisconsin day, and all the church windows were open.

"Go home and get your lunch!"

You guessed it! The noon whistle blew, and before we could realize what was happening, Dana stood up in the pew, turned toward the three hundred plus people in the congregation, and shouted, "Go home and get your lunch!"

Do I have to tell you? Church was over at that very moment. No benediction and no seven-fold amen!

Later Dad Buchanan, who had the world's best sense of humor, said, "It wouldn't have been so bad had not half the congregation shouted amen!"

Dealing with the Perfect Child

Becky Freeman

Once we had determined I would go back to college to finish my degree, the next question became, "What did I want to be other than a mom?" What were my talents other than cooking for a crowd? Like a good mother, I discussed it with the children, and one evening around the dinner table we went on to discuss toward what heights *they* might be aspiring.

Zach wavered between being a priest or a ballerina, which I thought was interesting since we are neither Catholic nor coordinated.

Zeke's answer took me somewhat aback, given his gentle nature, "An enemy," he responded firmly. (Hey—it'll sure save on those pesky college tuition bills.)

Turning to Rachel, I posed the question in a neutral-gendered, designed-to-encourage-nonstereotypical-thinking manner: "Would

you like to be a doctor or a nurse when you grow up?" After much thought, she replied in true feminist form.

"I'll have to wait and see which outfit looks better on me."

I'm beginning to feel I'm failing somewhere in this area because when I asked Zeke the question, "Why do we treat women with respect?" he answered sincerely, "Because you never know when you might need to use one."

Having drawn a blank in my quest for a career direction, I agreed to teach VBS that summer, which I have since learned can often stand for Very Bad Situation. One morning, I happened to stroll by the church kitchen with a preschooler named James by the hand. The aroma of fresh baked goods deliciously perfumed the air, and seeking to make conversation with James, I remarked,

"Why does my finger gots two elbows?"

"Mmmmm…what is that wonderful smell?"

James obviously possessed an esteem for his small self that needed no boosting. "It's me!" he beamed.

I loved it, and of course all the other moms loved it when I reported it to them, and that night, inspired by James, I sat down with my dog-eared journal and chuckled over the long list of questions I'd been asked at different times by my own or by other people's children.

"Mom, how do they make snakes turn into rubber?"

"What are those minnows that come in a can and that people eat?"

"Why does my finger gots two elbows?"

"Is your lap just for babies tonight?" (An excellent postpartum guilt inducer!)

"How do they squeeze people into those tiny airplanes up in the sky?"

"Are you potty-trained, Mom?"

"Can I have ice cream with chocolate chipmunks?"

"Will you put this up, Mom? I'm afraid I'm about to get into it."

"Why don't you just buy that zucchini swimsuit and let's get out of this lady store?" (Because I would need enough material to make a tent for the entire Saudi desert in order to cover up the stretch marks you gave me five years ago, thank you.)

Last but not least, as Gabe observed his first caterpillar, "What is this worm doing with a sweater on?"

I know that you have been waiting breathlessly for the chapter dealing with, "Raising the Difficult Child," or "How To Contain Your Little Warmonger." Actually, I feel uniquely qualified to discuss the problem of "Dealing with the Perfect Child," which Zeke just about is.

He did not begin life that way. He was born just eighteen months after Zach and got off to a terrible start. He had colic and cried for hours at night, even though I breast-fed him and rocked him and did all the right mother-things I knew to do. I did find some comfort in a book by Anne Ortlund, *Your Children Are Wet Cement*. My mother spotted the book on the kitchen table one evening as she walked the floor with screaming Zeke.

"Are you sure that's not, *Put Your Children in Wet Cement?*" she inquired.

As Zeke became a toddler, he was like a spider monkey, able to shinny up my legs and into my arms, clinging to my neck twenty-four hours a day, seven days a week it seemed, screaming most of the time.

Finally, one morning Mother called when I was at wit's end, drowning in a sea of tears and wondering if I would ever be able to enjoy this unhappy baby. I began to wail my misgivings and then noticed the other end of the line was very quiet, which to say the least, was unusual.

"Becky," she began, and I seemed to hear something akin to awe in her voice, "something happened this morning as I was praying for you and Zekey Baby that doesn't happen to me very often. It was as if the Lord shot a message into my head. It was very clear. It was, Zeke will be Becky's blessing."

Needless to say, I took heart, and have lived to see that prophecy more than fulfilled. This is the child who received the "Most Tenderhearted" award three times in a row in school. The little guy inherited bad teeth and suffered too much for his age in the dentist's chair, yet when he overheard me complain about the high dental bills, he told me earnestly, "I'll ask the dentist not to give me a prize next time so he won't charge you so much."

Zeke loves to work alongside his Dad, has patience beyond his years with other family members, and usually gives in to their desires. He will ride happily in the car for hours, and his favorite hobby is *reading!*

I had actually begun to worry about him until I overheard a conversation between him and his older brother and younger sister. Gabe was napping and the older three were sitting around a picnic table on the back porch enjoying the breeze from the lake. I was enjoying the fact that they were all sitting. They were growing so fast, it gave me a chance to look them over carefully and see what time was doing. Where had my babies gone?

Zach was so obviously an Arnold—stocky, deeply tanned,

straight dark brown hair, dark dancing eyes. Zeke, a total oppo-
site, was so obviously a Freeman—lanky, with light brown hair,
tender brown eyes, quiet and soft-spoken. And Rachel Praise?—
light brown curls, freckled, with an upturned nose, fair
skin…What long recessive gene pool had she drawn from to be
another totally different child? Whichever it was, Gabe had
dipped from the same pool for his fair skin and freckles, but
checked in at the Arnold's Spanish stream for his almost black
hair. But it looks like his build is going to be the best from the
Freeman pool, long, and lean with broad shoulders.

In my meditative state, I smiled as I thought of how relieved
Mother must be with the physical makeup of her grandchildren.

Years back, when she had realized Scott and I were headed
for the altar, she had worried about our progeny. "Becky dear,"
she had asked, "what if your children inherit the Arnold legs and
the Freeman arms?"

I had to admit—if the unthinkable happened, we might produce
a line of humans with the posture of a gorilla, but we were so in love
we were willing to risk it. There on the deck that gorgeous day I
knew our worries had been groundless. They were all fine looking
specimens. I was delighted with them, and with the moment.

I hadn't been paying much attention to their conversation,
but Zach made a pronouncement that caught my ear.

"I'm special because I'm the oldest," he said with pride.

Rachel quickly countered, "But I'm Daddy's sweetheart
because I'm the only girl." Both turned to Zeke who thought for
a moment, grinned, and assumed a saint-like expression.

"Yes, but *I'm* perfect," he intoned.

No one raised a voice to contradict him.

Contributors

Marti Attoun is a weekly humor columnist for her hometown newspaper, the *Joplin* (Mo.) *Globe,* and has published hundreds of articles in regional and national publications, including *Reader's Digest, Redbook,* the *Christian Science Monitor,* and *Family Circle.*

Charlene Ann Baumbich is an author, speaker, and humorist who invites readers to drop by www.dontmissyourlife.com. She lives in Glen Ellyn, Illinois, with her husband, George.

Martha Bolton is a former staff writer for Bob Hope, two-time Angel Award recipient, Emmy nominee, and the author of more than thirty books, including *Didn't My Skin Used to Fit?* and the "Official" Book Series.

Sue Buchanan is the author of several books, including *Duh-Votions* and *I'm Alive and the Doctor's Dead.* She co-wrote *Friends through Thick and Thin* and *Confessions of Friends through Thick and Thin* with Gloria Gaither, Peggy Benson, and Joy MacKenzie. She lives with her husband, Wayne, in Nashville.

Phil Callaway is a popular speaker and the author of numerous best-sellers, including *Who Put the Skunk in the Trunk?* and *I Used to Have Answers, Now I Have Kids.* Visit Phil's Web site at www.philcallaway.ab.ca.

Patsy Clairmont, a featured speaker at Women of Faith conferences, is the author of numerous best-selling books, including *God Uses Cracked Pots, Normal Is Just a Setting on Your Dryer,* and *Sportin' a 'Tude.*

Sharon Colwell is a freelance writer who has worked for Christianity Today International. She and her husband have enjoyed God's gift of their marriage for more than thirty years. They are blessed with two daughters, a son-in-law, and three grandsons and enjoy being active members of Living Hope Church in Elk Grove Village, Illinois.

G. Ron Darbee is the author of *Wrestling for the Remote Control* and *The Lord Is My Shepherd and I'm About to Be Sheared!* His award-winning short stories have been published in a wide range of publications.

Gwendolyn Mitchell Diaz has been a featured writer for several national magazines and is the author of *The Adventures of Mighty Mom* and *Mighty Mom's Secrets for Raising Super Kids.* She and her husband, Ed, are the parents of four sons.

Susan Duke is a best-selling author, inspirational speaker, and singer. She coauthored several titles, including *Courage for the Chicken-Hearted* and *Heartlifters for Women,* as well as the God Things Come in Small Packages series. She speaks at conferences, seminars, and churches nationwide.

Becky Freeman is an in-demand speaker and the best-selling author of numerous titles including the best-selling *Worms in My Tea* (coauthored with her mother Ruthie Arnold), *Peanut Butter Kisses and Mud Pie Hugs,* and *Chocolate Chili Pepper Love.* She and her husband, Scott, live in Greenville, Texas, with their four children.

Kathi Hunter is a popular retreat speaker and freelance writer whose work has appeared in numerous publications, including *Today's Christian Woman* and *Focus on the Family.* She and her husband, Paul, live in San Jose, California, with their two children.

Susan Friday Lamb is a communications specialist at the North Carolina Museum of History in Raleigh. She enjoys spending time with her husband, Terry, and two daughters, Elizabeth and Emily.

Contributors

Karen Scalf Linamen is the author of numerous books, including *Just Hand Over the Chocolate and No One Will Get Hurt*. She is a contributing editor for *Today's Christian Woman* magazine and the author of more than one hundred magazine articles. Karen also speaks frequently at churches, women's retreats, and writers' conferences.

Gracie Malone is a conference and retreat speaker, freelance writer, and Bible-study teacher. Her articles have been published in numerous publications, including *Discipleship Journal, Moody,* and *Christian Parenting Today*. She and her husband, Joe, have three sons and six grandchildren.

Dan N. "Max" Mayhew is a minister, freelance writer, and a former high-school teacher. His mostly humorous writing appears regularly in several Northwest publications. The Mayhews live in Portland, Oregon, near several households among the Summit Fellowships, a home-church community.

Marilyn Meberg, a popular Women of Faith conference speaker, is the author of numerous titles including the best-selling *I'd Rather Be Laughing* and *Choosing the Amusing*. She lives in Palm Desert, California.

Helen Widger Middlebrooke is the mother of nine and the author of *Lessons for a Super Mom: Devotions from the Middle of Life*.

Chonda Pierce is a popular speaker, comedian, author, and singer. Her work includes the books *It's Always Darkest before the Fun Comes Up, Chonda Pierce on Her Soapbox, I Can See Myself in His Eyeballs,* the video *Chonda Pierce on Her Soapbox,* and the music CD *Yes...and Amen*. She lives in Nashville, Tennessee.

Fran Caffey Sandin is the author of *See You Later, Jeffrey* and a contributor to *The Strength of a Woman*. Her articles have been published widely in such publications as *Moody, Virtue, Focus on the Family Physician,* and *Home Life*. She and her husband, James, are the parents of three grown children.

Sheri Rose Shepherd is a popular conference speaker and national spokesperson for Teen Challenge. She is the author of several titles, including *Fit for Excellence, 7 Ways to Build a Better You,* and *Life Is Not a Dress Rehearsal*. Sheri leads Foundation for Excellence Ministries from her home in Oregon, where she lives with her husband and two children.

Stan Toler is the senior pastor of Trinity Church of the Nazarene in Oklahoma City. He is the author of several titles, including *The Buzzards Are Circling, but God's Not Finished with Me Yet* and *God Has Never Failed Me, but He's Sure Scared Me to Death a Few Times.*

Laura Jensen Walker is a popular public speaker and author whose works include *Dated Jekyll, Married Hyde* and *Love Handles for the Romantically Impaired.* She and her husband live in northern California.

Lynn Bowen Walker is a freelance writer whose work has appeared in numerous periodicals, including *Marriage Partnership, Christian Parenting Today, Moody, Glamour,* and *American Baby.* She and her husband, Mark, live in Los Gatos, California, and are the parents of two sons.

LeAnn Weiss is the coauthor of *God Things Come in Small Packages for Women* (with Susan Duke and Judy Carden) and *God Things Come in Small Packages for Moms* (with Duke, Carden, and Caron Chandler Loveless).

Patricia Wilson is a speaker and the author of numerous titles, including *Too Much Holly, Not Enough Holy? The Daisies Are Still Free,* and *How Can I Be over the Hill When I Haven't Seen the Top Yet?* She lives with her husband and children in rural Ontario, Canada.

Source Notes

chapter 1: laugh and the whole world laughs...

"When a Chicken Goes to Church" excerpt taken from *Courage for the Chicken Hearted*. Copyright 1998 by Becky Freeman, Susan Duke, Rebecca Barlow Jordan, Gracie Malone & Fran Caffey Sandin. Used by permission of RiverOak Publishing, Tulsa, OK. All rights reserved.

"Hens and Neighbors Gather 'Round" excerpt taken from *Courage for the Chicken Hearted*. Copyright 1998 by Becky Freeman, Susan Duke, Rebecca Barlow Jordan, Gracie Malone & Fran Caffey Sandin. Used by permission of RiverOak Publishing, Tulsa, OK. All rights reserved.

"Loony 'Tudes" taken from *Sportin' a 'Tude* by Patsy Clairmont, a Focus on the Family book published by Tyndale House Publishers. Copyright © 1996 by Patsy Clairmont. All rights reserved. International copyright secured. Used by permission.

chapter 2: the mother of all laughs

"You Know You're Really a Parent When..." by Susan Friday Lamb. This article first appeared in *Christian Parenting Today* magazine

(July/August 1998), a publication of Christianity Today, Inc. Used by permission.

"Paging Dr. Mom" taken from *Don't Miss Your Kids* by Charlene Ann Baumbich. Copyright © 1991 by Charlene Ann Baumbich. Used by permission of InterVarsity Press, P.O. Box 1400, Downers Grove, IL 60515. www.ivpress.com

"A Jiggling Box of Joy" taken from *God Things Come in Small Packages for Moms* by LeAnn Weiss. Copyright © 2000. Starburst Publishers, Lancaster, PA 17601. Used by permission. www.starburstpublishers.com

chapter 3: laugh your way to a better figure

"Who Me? Sweat?!?" by Lynn Bowen Walker. Used by permission.

"Chicken 'n' Dumplings" excerpt taken from *Eggstra Courage for the Chicken Hearted.* Copyright 1999 by Becky Freeman, Susan Duke, Rebecca Barlow Jordan, Gracie Malone & Fran Caffey Sandin. Used by permission of RiverOak Publishing, Tulsa, OK. All rights reserved.

"Club Sweat" taken from *Mama Said There'd Be Days Like This* by Charlene Ann Baumbich. Copyright © 1995. Servant Publications, Ann Arbor, MI. Used by permission.

chapter 4: making humor your hobby

"Time to Unravel a Sweater Mystery" by Marti Attoun. Used by permission.

"How to Break All the Rules (and Still Throw a Great Party)" by Lynn Bowen Walker. This article first appeared in the Spring, 1995 issue of *Marriage Partnership*.

"Family Antiques Expert" by Marti Attoun. Marti Attoun has published hundreds of articles in national publications and lives in Joplin, Missouri. Used by permission.

chapter 5: queen of domesticity

"Vanamaniacs: Mom's Checklist to Know When to Clean Out the Van" by Kathi Hunter. Used by permission.

"Keeping the Home Fires Burning" taken from *God Things Come in Small Packages for Women* by Susan Duke. Copyright © 2000. Used by

permission, Starburst Publishers, Lancaster, PA 17604. www.starburst-publishers.com

"The Sunday Morning Comics (and Other Indispensable Gardening Tools)" taken from *Welcome to the Funny Farm* by Karen Scalf Linamen. Copyright © 2001. Used by permission, Fleming H. Revell, a division of Baker Book House Company.

chapter 6: looking fine, feeling foolish

"Say Good-bye to Good Intentions" taken from *Welcome to the Funny Farm* by Karen Scalf Linamen. Copyright © 2001. Used by permission, Fleming H. Revell, a division of Baker Book House Company.

"Celebrating the Unexpected!" Sue Buchanan, copyright © 2001, W Publishing Group, Nashville, Tennessee. All rights reserved.

"Only My UPS Man Knows for Sure," taken from *God Things Come in Small Packages for Women* by Susan Duke. Copyright © 2000. Used by permission, Starburst Publishers, Lancaster, PA 17604. www.starburstpublishers.com

chapter 7: clutter bugs unite!

"Checks and Unbalances" taken from *If You Can't Stand the Smoke, Stay Out of My Kitchen* by Martha Bolton. Copyright © 1990. Used by permission, Beacon Hill Press of Kansas City.

"It May Be Chaos, but It's Mine" taken from *Mama Said There'd Be Days Like This* by Charlene Ann Baumbich. Copyright © 1995. Servant Publications, Ann Arbor, MI. Used by permission.

"Clutter Management 101" taken from *Welcome to the Funny Farm* by Karen Scalf Linamen. Copyright © 2001. Used by permission, Fleming H. Revell, a division of Baker Book House Company.

chapter 8: laughter for the chronologically challenged

"Betty's Mother" is taken from *How Can I Be Over the Hill When I Haven't Seen the Top Yet?* Copyright © 1989 by Patricia Wilson. Used by permission of Upper Room Books, Nashville, Tennessee.

"Mentalpause" taken from *Mentalpause...and Other Midlife Laughs* by Laura Jensen Walker. Copyright © 2001. Used by permission, Fleming H. Revell, a division of Baker Book House Company.

"How Did You Get So Old?" from *Lessons for a Super Mom* by Helen Widger Middlebrooke, published by Barbour Books, an imprint of Barbour Publishing, Inc., Uhrichsville, Ohio. Used by permission.

chapter 9: technology: friend or foe?

"Techno Babble" taken from *Mama Said There'd Be Days Like This* by Charlene Ann Baumbich. Copyright © 1995. Servant Publications, Ann Arbor, MI. Used by permission.

"Caller I.Q." Marilyn Meberg, copyright © 2002, W Publishing Group, Nashville, Tennessee. All rights reserved.

"More Things, More Holders" by Marti Attoun. Used by permission.

chapter 10: a pound of laughter

"Weighty Matters" taken from *God Uses Cracked Pots* by Patsy Clairmont, a Focus on the Family book published by Tyndale House Publishers. Copyright © 1991 by Patsy Clairmont. All rights reserved. International copyright secured. Used by permission.

"Crash Diet at Freeway Speeds" taken from *Welcome to the Funny Farm* by Karen Scalf Linamen. Copyright © 2001. Used by permission, Fleming H. Revell, a division of Baker Book House Company.

"George and Charlene in the Garden of Calories" taken from *Mama Said There'd Be Days Like This* by Charlene Ann Baumbich. Copyright © 1995. Servant Publications, Ann Arbor, MI. Used by permission.

chapter 11: mama mia—more humor for moms

"Germs of Endearment" taken from *Peanut Butter Kisses and Mudpie Hugs.* Copyright 2000 by Becky Freeman. Published by Harvest House Publishers, Eugene, OR. Used by permission.

"The Great Diaper Derby" taken from I CAN SEE MYSELF IN HIS EYEBALLS by Chonda Pierce. Copyright © 2001 by Chonda Pierce. Used by permission of Zondervan.

"White Can Wait" excerpt taken from *The Adventures of Mighty Mom.* Copyright 2000 by Gwendolyn Mitchell Diaz. Used by permission of RiverOak Publishing, Tulsa, OK. All rights reserved.

chapter 12: adolescent amusement

"Know When to Say No, Part 1" from *Lessons for a Super Mom* by Helen Widger Middlebrooke, published by Barbour Books, an imprint of Barbour Publishing, Inc., Uhrichsville, Ohio. Used by permission.

"Cats Can't Baby-sit" excerpt taken from *The Adventures of Mighty Mom.* Copyright 2000 by Gwendolyn Mitchell Diaz. Used by permission of RiverOak Publishing, Tulsa, OK. All rights reserved.

"Know When to Say No, Part 2" from *Lessons for a Super Mom* by Helen Widger Middlebrooke, published by Barbour Books, an imprint of Barbour Publishing, Inc., Uhrichsville, Ohio. Used by permission.

chapter 13: funny honeys

"23 Ways to Amuse Yourself during Football Season" by Lynn Bowen Walker. Used by permission.

"Forget Marriage Seminars—Try Wallpapering" by Sharon Colwell. This article first appeared in *Marriage Partnership* magazine (Fall 2000), a publication of Christianity Today, Inc. Used by permission.

"Fixin' Stuff" taken from *Milk & Cookies to Make You Smile.* Copyright 2002 by Becky Freeman. Published by Harvest House Publishers, Eugene, OR. Used by permission.

chapter 14: man-oh-man

"Little Henry Sounds Off" by Dan N. "Max" Mayhew. Copyright © 1999 Max Features. This article first appeared in *Portland Family* magazine (January 2000). Used by permission.

"Of Things Green and Slimy" taken from *Wrestling for the Remote Control* by G. Ron Darbee. Copyright © 1996. All rights reserved. Published by Broadman & Holman Publishers, Nashville, Tennessee. Used by permission.

"Pop Quiz" taken from *Who Put My Life on Fast-Forward?* (Harvest House) by Phil Callaway. Copyright © 2002. Used by permission. www.philcallaway.com

chapter 15: women and cheese

"Playing Connect-the-Dots with My Age Spots" taken from *Mentalpause...and Other Midlife Laughs* by Laura Jensen Walker. Copyright © 2001. Used by permission, Fleming H. Revell, a division of Baker Book House Company.

"Top Ten Signs You're Growing More Mature" excerpt taken from *The Buzzards Are Circling, but God's Not Finished with Me Yet.* Copyright 2001 by Stan Toler. Used by permission of RiverOak Publishing, Tulsa, OK. All rights reserved.

"The Middle-Age Top 40 Chart" taken from *Mentalpause...and Other Midlife Laughs* by Laura Jensen Walker. Copyright © 2001. Used by permission, Fleming H. Revell, a division of Baker Book House Company.

chapter 16: just when you thought it was safe

"Security Blanket" excerpted from *Life Is Not a Dress Rehearsal* © 2000 by Sheri Rose Shepherd. Used by permission of Multnomah Publishers, Inc.

"Accidental Perspective" taken from *Normal Is Just a Setting on Your Dryer* by Patsy Clairmont, a Focus on the Family book published by Tyndale House Publishers. Copyright © 1993 by Patsy Clairmont. All rights reserved. International copyright secured. Used by permission.

"True Grace," taken from *God Things Come in Small Packages for Women* by Susan Duke. Copyright © 2000. Used by permission, Starburst Publishers, Lancaster, PA 17604. www.starburstpublishers.com

chapter 17: kids: God's way of making sure we laugh

"How to Speak 'Kid'" from *Lessons for a Super Mom* by Helen Widger Middlebrooke, published by Barbour Books, an imprint of Barbour Publishing, Inc., Uhrichsville, Ohio. Used by permission.

"We Thought They Were Asleep Till They Said Amen" taken from DUH-VOTIONS by Sue Buchanan. Copyright © 1999 by Sue Buchanan. Used by permission of Zondervan.

"Dealing with the Perfect Child" taken from *Worms in My Tea* by Becky Freeman and Ruthie Arnold. Copyright © 1994. Used by permission, Broadman & Holman Publishers, Nashville, TN. All rights reserved.